Penetration Testing

Protecting networks and systems

Penetration Testing

Protecting networks and systems

KEVIN M. HENRY

IT Governance Publishing

Every possible effort has been made to ensure that the information contained in this book is accurate at the time of going to press, and the publisher and the author cannot accept responsibility for any errors or omissions, however caused. Any opinions expressed in this book are those of the author, not the publisher. Websites identified are for reference only, not endorsement, and any website visits are at the reader's own risk. No responsibility for loss or damage occasioned to any person acting, or refraining from action, as a result of the material in this publication can be accepted by the publisher or the author.

Apart from any fair dealing for the purposes of research or private study, or criticism or review, as permitted under the Copyright, Designs and Patents Act 1988, this publication may only be reproduced, stored or transmitted, in any form, or by any means, with the prior permission in writing of the publisher or, in the case of reprographic reproduction, in accordance with the terms of licences issued by the Copyright Licensing Agency. Enquiries concerning reproduction outside those terms should be sent to the publisher at the following address:

IT Governance Publishing
IT Governance Limited
Unit 3, Clive Court
Bartholomew's Walk
Cambridgeshire Business Park
Ely
Cambridgeshire
CB7 4EA
United Kingdom

www.itgovernance.co.uk

First published in the United Kingdom in 2012
by IT Governance Publishing.

ISBN 978-1-84928-371-7

PREFACE

This book is a combination of attacking and defending. It is an attempt to shed light on the thoughts, motivations and actions of an attacker against an organization or individual, so that each of us can better defend our systems, our intellectual property and our values. Part of a good defense is a strong offense – and knowing how to probe, test and strengthen our systems is also knowing how to test and evaluate the effectiveness of our security controls and the resilience of our systems.

To become a great penetration tester requires experience and skill. It involves creativity, persistence and patience. This book discusses the management and planning side of penetration testing. It is not focused on how to use the tools available – tools change and new ones come out continuously – but rather the timeless managerial and planning skills needed to plan, conduct and report on the security of a system, network, organization and its people. Mix this knowledge with hours learning the tools, and you will be well on your way to understanding how to make a difference to the security, reliability and resilience of your organization.

ABOUT THE AUTHOR

Kevin Henry has been working on computer systems for over 35 years. He began as an operator on the largest mini-computer installation in Canada in the mid 1970s and has since worked as a programmer, analyst, auditor and security expert. He currently provides security auditing, training and educational programs for major clients and governments around the world and is a frequent speaker at major security conferences.

Kevin lives with his wife and children in Blumenort, Manitoba, Canada, where winters are cold, and people are always friendly and helpful.

ACKNOWLEDGEMENTS

The author would like to thank Ray Friedman, Steve Mayes, Keyvan Ejtemai and Marc Thompson for their support and the opportunities they have provided over the years.

We would like to acknowledge the following reviewers of this book for their useful contributions: Jared Carstensen, Manager, Deloitte & Touche, Tiago Henriques and Antonio Velasco, CEO, Sinersys Technologies.

This book is dedicated to Rosalyn. I cannot thank her enough for her support and care – she is truly a Pearl beyond price.

CONTENTS

Contents

INTRODUCTION

Today's world runs on technology. Nearly every business benefits from – and relies on – technology in one form or another. The use of technology has brought tremendous advantages to society by making services, features and knowledge more readily available than ever before. We can communicate across the planet (and, in fact, across the universe) in seconds, and can effectively control millions of devices instantly – something we could never have done previously through simple human action.

The use of technology also, however, presents several risks to society. By using it, we develop a greater reliance on devices that lack the sense of judgment and discriminatory thought that a knowledgeable person would have. Such devices may provide us with erroneous data and cause us to make incorrect assumptions, errors in judgment or action, and possibly even seriously injure or harm society, finances and individuals.

To correctly deploy technology is a serious challenge – one that requires constant education, practice and testing. Moreover, the use of technology must always be seen in context. Technology is not an end in itself, it is not the magic answer to every problem, and it should never be implemented just for the sake of using a new tool or because it is available. Technology has one purpose, and that is to support the mission or objectives of the user/organization. As we will see through this book, the proper use of technology starts long before the technology itself is purchased. It starts with defining the business objectives and then designing the best solution for to meeting those objectives.

Despite the best intentions of designers, architects, developers and operations staff, technology is still subject to failure, breaches and compromise. Equipment, processes and people require careful monitoring and regular testing to ensure that the systems, networks, applications, security equipment and other technologies are working in a secure, reliable manner, and that they are not presenting new opportunities for attack against the organization.

Testing is the key to providing assurance of the correct implementation and operation of technology, and this book will examine the skills and techniques used by a professional penetration tester to provide the accurate, thorough and meaningful reports that their clients or management teams need on the secure operation of systems and equipment.

CHAPTER 1: INTRODUCTION TO PENETRATION TESTING

Penetration testing captures the imagination and sparks the interests of many people. It is part mystery, part challenge, part creativity and part risk. It has the glamour and mystique of doing something on the wild side of life by simulating a criminal act, but without the penalties. Therefore, it is no surprise that many people are drawn to penetration testing and want to know more about what it is, how to do it and, moreover, how they can use it to help protect their systems and defend their networks.

Protecting the systems and networks of today requires a broad understanding and in-depth knowledge of the tactics, tools and motivations of the adversary. The person given the responsibility to protect a system should know the nature and techniques of the enemy, and be able to prevent successful attacks by discovering and securing any vulnerabilities in their systems or networks before the adversary can find them.

Penetration testing is the simulation of an attack on a system, network, piece of equipment or other facility, with the objective of proving how vulnerable that system or "target" would be to a real attack.

Penetration testing is based on knowledge. The more knowledge the tester has, the more effective their attack will likely be. But what knowledge do they need? They need knowledge about the target, the operating environment, the users, the culture, the business itself, the physical security and, most of all, knowledge of how to use the tools (and their imagination) effectively.

Many people have a narrow and limited perception of penetration testing; they see it as an attack using a few common tools against a list of commonly known vulnerabilities. This type of testing provides some benefit to the organization, but is far too superficial and restrained to be really effective and meaningful. A pen test is innovative, probing, testing, evaluative, persistent and thorough.

In this booklet, we will examine various types of penetration tests, the tools commonly used, and the ways to leverage a pen test to provide the greatest possible benefit to the organization. The resulting penetration tests will deliver assurance and confidence to clients and business owners that their systems, networks and facilities are secure, that the level of risk to the organization of an attack is within acceptable levels, and that their information systems are being managed properly.

Case study

The General responsible for overseeing the security and operations of a military network requested a penetration test. The General was convinced that his network was secure, well-hidden and impenetrable. He had diligently instructed his staff to ensure that the network was well managed, unnecessary services were disabled, and that no extraneous information about the network was available anywhere outside of the network itself. He hired a top-quality pen testing team and challenged them to enter his network, but, at the same time, was convinced they would not even find it, let alone gain enough knowledge to launch a proper attack.

A couple of weeks into the test schedule, the pen testing team requested a meeting with the General. As he entered the meeting, the General asked if they had "given up already." The team then laid in front of the General the information they had managed to access, and stated that they were required to cease the test once they had obtained such information under the rules of the engagement. (Note: these rules must be set out at the beginning of the test, since there may be serious implications and potential damage to the organization once the testing team has gained access – especially when succeeding in penetrating a military network.)

Upon reviewing the documents obtained by the pen testing team, the General exploded in rage, demanding to know how they had managed to obtain so much sensitive, classified material. He threatened to demote his entire technical team and launch a legal investigation into his department. It was at this point that the pen testing team advised the General that the General's network was quite secure, and that the way they broke into the network was not through a sophisticated technical attack. They were able to access all of the information by simply sending a DVD that contained a Trojan horse to the General himself. When inserted into the General's machine, the Trojan promptly copied the entire contents of the hard drive on the General's machine to a secure server that the pen testing team had set up.

They delivered the DVD to the General using a journalist that had an interview with him to discuss a news article being written about technology in today's military. The DVD contained video clips and articles as a sample of the work that the journalist had already done to prepare the article.

Such an attack should not have been successful – no foreign media should have been installed onto a classified machine, and both policies and technical controls should have prevented this. But what happens in reality? Many people, including Generals, senior managers and even technical staff, could fall for such an easy trick.

As can be seen in this case, there are many challenges involved in carrying out a successful pen test. The first is to gain approval to conduct the test, the second is to determine the rules of engagement, the third is to know the reporting structure and who to deliver the results to, the fourth is to ensure the pen test is not limited to a strictly technical attack and, finally, the fifth is to ensure that the test provides meaningful results and recommendations for the organization.

We all know that most organizations would fall for such an attack. There is no technical control that is sufficient to totally prevent user mistakes! The 2011 attacks against RSA (the security division of the EMC) are an example of how easy it can be to penetrate even the most security-conscious organization. In the case of RSA, the exploit was enabled through a simple spear phishing e-mail sent to an employee. The employee opened the attachment that was linked to the e-mail (which promised them a list of open employment positions) and thereby launched the hacking tool that provided a backdoor into the company for the attacker to use[1].

---

[1] *http://www.f-secure.com/weblog/archives/00002226.html*.

The purpose of a pen test is to find any problems on the system and network, and in the user training, business procedures and operational controls related to the system being tested. A successful pen test is one that discovers the vulnerabilities and determines the level of risk they pose to the organization. An unsuccessful pen test is one where the team fails to find existing serious vulnerabilities and provides management with a false assurance of security, or one that provides the organization with a flood of meaningless data that is not sorted according to priorities or levels of risk.

The many breaches that Sony experienced in 2011 were mostly the result of simple attacks. The vulnerabilities that allowed the attacks to do the damage and compromise those systems affected should have been found by competent pen testers and thereby corrected. The Verizon-USSS data breach report of 2010 indicated that 96% of all data breaches were avoidable through simple or intermediate controls[2]. This is where many pen tests are failing. The pen tester bears the responsibility to perform their duties in a professional and competent manner, and thereby provide the information required by their clients to strengthen and secure their systems and networks.

Security basics

Penetration testing is a process of testing and validating the security posture and maturity of an organization. In order to test the security program, it is necessary for the pen tester to know what to look for and what the security priorities are.

---

[2] *http://securityblog.verizonbusiness.com.*

The first problem is that the term "security" is an abstract term and can mean many different things to different people.

Definition

One resource[3] defines security in the following ways:

1. Freedom from danger, risk, etc.; safety
2. Freedom from care, anxiety, or doubt; well-founded confidence
3. Something that secures or makes safe; protection; defense
4. Freedom from financial cares or from want
5. Precautions taken to guard against crime, attack, sabotage, espionage, etc.

We can see many positive aspects of security – freedom from worry and danger, for example – but we also see that security is very much an emotional term, conveying a sense of safety and protection. The last definition is most relevant for us: "precautions taken to guard."

A pen tester is not testing emotion or a feeling of safety; the tester is testing the precautions, the defenses and the levels of risk or danger.

The information security triad

For many years, the information security industry has defined the term "security" as comprising three core

---

[3] *http://dictionary.reference.com.*

elements: *confidentiality*, *integrity* and *availability*. There are good reasons for this. Using these three elements to define security gives a more complete picture, and provides a way to move the term away from an abstract, emotion-based meaning to one denoting something solid and measureable.

Figure 1: The CIA triad

Confidentiality

Confidentiality is based on confidence – trust and assurance that the organization is protecting sensitive information and systems from unauthorized access and disclosure. This requires the organization to *know* what information it has that requires protection. It starts with the classification of systems and data according to the level of damage that

The objective of an attacker is not just to prove that they can get access. They want something. They want the organization's sensitive data, and they want continued access; they want to "own" the systems and networks of the organization for their own benefit. The pen tester must, therefore, see the objectives of the test as evaluating the ability of the organization to resist compromise, detecting an intrusion, and mitigating any damage that results from an intrusion.

The pen tester is testing the security of the system and ensuring that the core assets of the organization are protected from compromise.

Testing for confidentiality, therefore, is testing whether an unauthorized person can gain access to the organization's systems and data, and whether an authorized person may be able to commit unauthorized acts.

Integrity

"Integrity" refers to the accuracy and precision of data and systems processing. When an organization relies on the accuracy of data – or the reliability of a process – it must be confident of the integrity of that data and process and prevent improper modification or alteration of that data or process, whether through error, malicious activity or equipment malfunction.

A pen test is always a test conducted at a point in time, but the pen tester must still ensure that the data is not only accurate at the time of the test, but that the controls are adequate to protect it from improper modification in the future, as well. This would mean testing for the ability to make a change or alter a process in a way, or by a person, that should not have been permitted.

Availability

In today's world of rapid business operations, where decisions must be made both quickly and accurately, the availability of systems and data must also be assured. Where users and customers rely on systems providing data and service in a real-time mode, an outage may have catastrophic consequences. For many organizations, it is simply not good enough to tell customers that their systems are down or that the data they require is currently not available.

The main point is that not all systems and data have the same importance – some systems are critical, while others are simply "nice to have." Air traffic control systems are extremely critical (as long as the airport is operational), but an automated teller machine (ATM) or automated banking machine (ABM) is not nearly as important. The failure of an ATM is an inconvenience; the failure of air traffic control – for even a few moments – may result in extreme loss of life. Therefore, there is no security solution that is suitable for every need. Each business must tailor its security solution according to factors including the law, customer expectations, financial impact and reputation. When testing the security of an organization and its susceptibility to failure or compromise, the pen tester must relate the tests and the test results to the operational and security environment the organization works in.

The yardstick

By using confidentiality, integrity and availability as yardsticks, an organization can measure how well they are doing (their current level of security) against their desired position (where they need/want to be). Availability, for example, is an excellent yardstick. The organization will need to ask: what is the standard/level of availability the organization requires? How are they currently doing in comparison to that metric or standard? Are the systems and data of the organization meeting the required standard? Are they exceeding the desired standard? Or, are the current levels of availability substandard and inadequate? These questions are critically important, since they allow the organization to put a solid definition on what security means for them. A secure system is a system that provides the levels of confidentiality, availability and integrity required by the organization. Once the organization knows what those levels of security are, and whether or not it is meeting them, it can put in place the steps to address any security deficiencies and allocate the time, budget and resources required to implement its security program. This is why a pen test is so very important – it identifies the current security level of the organization, helps put together the plan to fix any vulnerabilities before an attacker finds those same vulnerabilities and makes the organization a victim of an attack.

The pen tester should not work strictly according to a template or checklist. A checklist is generic, and may be insensitive to the unique characteristics of the organization. Instead, the checklist should be used as a framework and then adjusted accordingly. The pen tester must understand the operational and security environment of the organization, and must measure the security against best practices, standards and the security position the organization is attempting to reach. Some organizations are more cautious than others; others have a larger risk appetite. The pen test must deliver an assessment that is sensitive to that operational environment.

Non-repudiation

Another area sometimes included in the CIA security triad is non-repudiation. Non-repudiation is a very important term in e-commerce and networked operations. Non-repudiation makes it possible to link an activity to its originator. It ensures that the person that initiated an activity would be unable to later deny that they were the person that committed that act. This would remove their option hide their identity and mask their activity. The pen tester will test the non-repudiation controls to determine whether an attacker would be able to erase log files, masquerade as another user, or set up false user accounts on the system to hide their activity.

Information classification

Not all information, and not all systems, require the same level of protection. Therefore, many organizations will set up a security classification scheme that will identify and label data according to the level of protection it needs. Information that requires higher levels of protection must be labeled and handled appropriately – according to how the data is stored, handled, transmitted, disposed of and displayed. The security controls must be adequate to protect sensitive information from unauthorized changes, disclosure and destruction, and the tests performed should ensure that the data protection controls are working correctly and cannot be easily circumvented by an attacker.

When is security enough?

The inevitable question is, "When is enough security enough?" There is no easy answer to this question. If an organization has had a breach, then there was not enough security – no matter how much they spent on it. If they have not had a breach, then there is always the suspicion that they are spending too much! Pen testers have a responsibility (and some may say a liability) to provide accurate and complete results to the client organization. They must ensure that they completed their work with due diligence and competence and have not provided false or misleading information to the client. There is no *one* answer to the "enough security" question, and all of the benchmarks and best practices represent only an attempt to define "adequate security." The pen tester must be able to defend the testing program they have set up. This is why the pen tester may want to base their tests on standards, such as the Payment Card Industry Data Security Standard (PCI DSS), ISO/IEC 27002 or COBIT,® or other such benchmarks.

Risk management

Risk management is the process that allows IT managers to balance the operational and economic costs of protective measures and achieve gains in mission capability by protecting the IT systems and data that support their organizations' missions.

Risk is a function of the likelihood of a given threat-source's exercising a particular potential vulnerability, and the resulting impact of that adverse event on the organization.

NIST SP 800-30[4]

We cannot avoid risk – but we must manage it. We operate in a world full of it, but risk is both danger and opportunity. Taking risks may lead to rewards; taking too much risk may lead to loss. In performing a pen test, the tester must understand the risk appetite of the organization: whether the organization tends to minimize risk or embrace it. IT risk is only a subset of business risk[5]. The danger for a technical pen tester is that they will forget that that risk must be measured, ultimately, from the perspective of the business, and not just in terms of IT-related risk.

As written in the ISO31000, organizations should develop, implement and continuously improve a framework whose purpose is to integrate the process for managing risk into the organization's overall governance, strategy and planning, management, reporting processes, policies, values and culture[6].

---

[4] *NIST SP 800-30: Risk Management Guide for Information Technology Systems* (2002), www.csrc.nist.gov/publications/drafts/800-30-rev1/SP800-30-Rev1-ipd.pdf.
[5] The Risk IT Framework, www.isaca.org.
[6] *ISO/IEC 31000:2009 – Risk management –Principles and guidelines.*

Risk justifies controls and controls should be traceable back to risk[7]. When planning and conducting a pen test, the tester must know the balance between security, risk, business and assurance.

Definitions[8]

- Threat: the potential for a threat source to exercise (accidentally trigger or intentionally exploit) a specific vulnerability.
- Threat source: either
    1. An intent and method targeted at the intentional exploitation of a vulnerability, or
    2. A situation and method that may accidentally trigger a vulnerability.
- Threat analysis: the examination of threat sources against system vulnerabilities to determine the threats for a particular system in a particular operational environment.
- Vulnerability: a flaw or weakness in system security procedures, design, implementation, or internal controls that could be exercised (accidentally triggered or intentionally exploited) and result in a security breach or a violation of the system's security policy.

---

[7] SABSA – Sherwood Applied Business Security Architecture, *www.sabsa.org*.
[8] *NIST SP800-30: Risk Management Guide for Information Technology Systems* (2002).

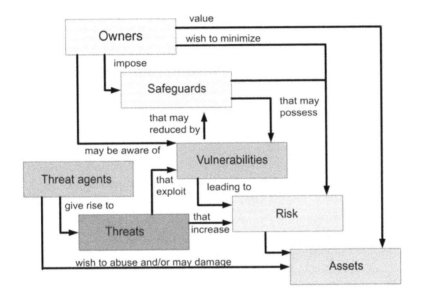

Figure 2: Risk management

The above graphic is from the Common Criteria[9] and is an excellent way to depict the process of risk management.

An asset is anything of value to its owner – including things both tangible (money, property, etc.) and intangible (reputation, confidence, etc.) While the owner wants to protect his assets, an attacker may pose the risk of abusing, damaging or destroying those assets. In order for the threat source to pose a legitimate threat, there must be a way for the threat source to cause the damage – the threat itself (a virus, physical access, equipment failure, etc.) Despite the presence of a threat (a virus, for example), an asset is still

---

[9] *www.commoncriteriaportal.org.*

not at risk unless there is some way for the threat to damage or gain access to the asset – a vulnerability. Therefore, we can see that a risk is a combination of three main elements: an asset, a threat and a vulnerability. Once the threats and vulnerabilities have been identified, the organization can deploy safeguards and countermeasures to reduce the risk. In nearly every case, it is impossible to eliminate or even reduce a threat – those are often beyond the control of the owner – but it *is* possible to mitigate the risk by reducing the vulnerability. For example, a virus is a threat written by a threat agent/source to exploit a vulnerability in an application. The owner deploys a patch that closes the vulnerability. This reduces the risk of that virus affecting that asset. It does not remove the threat or affect the threat agent, but it makes the owner's asset (the application) impervious to the threat. When conducting a pen test, the tester must understand how to identify assets that need protecting, what the threats to those assets are, and what vulnerabilities may exist in the management, technical or operational environment that may allow a threat agent to damage the asset and thereby pose a risk to it.

The threat environment

The environment that the systems and networks of each business operate in changes at an almost daily pace. New technologies are emerging; new methods of business are developing; and the methods of attack used by adversaries are improving – as is the skill and motivation of the attackers.

As every organization undergoes changes to its operations and infrastructure, new risks or opportunities emerge for the attacker. The technologies that enable improved business operations may also present new attack surfaces, introduce new vulnerabilities, and present the attacker with an opportunity to launch a pre-emptive strike before the target organization is ready. The attacker can launch new forms of attack against these technologies before the organization has managed to implement new controls, policies or operational procedures to deal with the new technology. The introduction of wireless internet, smartphones and SCADA® controls can create such a risk. Many organizations were exposed to the risks associated with the implementations of these tools long before they had determined the policies, procedures, standards and baseline configurations that should have been followed in bringing such technologies into the workplace. The same is happening today with web applications. Most organizations are just beginning to realize the risks and security requirements that are associated with developing and deploying web applications – especially those that handle sensitive data or support critical business functions. Insecure web applications are the attackers' treasure chest.

It is only by conducting regular pen tests and vulnerability assessments that the organization can ensure that their systems, applications and networks remain protected, and that the security controls and countermeasures that are in place are operating effectively.

Figure 3: Reasons to conduct a pen test

The ability of an attack to succeed is dependent on several factors: the vulnerabilities, skill and motivation of the attacker, and the presence of a legitimate threat capability (a tool that can be used in the attack). The more skilled and motivated the attacker is, the more likely they are to succeed. This is a threat in today's world especially, since many attackers are highly skilled and employed by organized criminal groups or foreign governments. This situation requires the pen tester to be all the more diligent in executing a thorough and skilled test and providing accurate, meaningful reports and recommendations to their clients.

Overview of the steps to penetration testing

A penetration test is not a disjointed series of random actions, but rather a targeted and carefully planned series of activities, which build on each other to create a successful attack. As stated earlier, the secret to penetration testing is knowledge: knowing the enemy, knowing the victim, knowing the tools and techniques, and knowing how to use those in an effective manner.

The steps to a penetration test can be defined as follows:

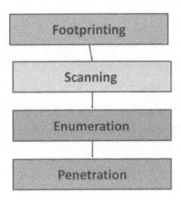

Figure 4: Steps to penetration testing

We can use the analogy of an attack against a medieval castle to make the steps to penetration testing simple and easy to understand.

Footprinting

The first step in attacking a castle is to learn about the castle. Describe it: what are its strengths, weaknesses, its behaviors and its level of alertness?

Footprinting is all about gathering as much information as possible about the target system. This would include determining the attack surfaces of the target system and documenting all the information available from public sources and from surreptitious tests.

Scanning

The second phase of attacking a castle will involve sending in spies and conducting more active searches of the target.

The attacker will now move on to the process of more active probing or scanning. This will highlight some of the characteristics of the system, including ports or services that are open.

Enumeration

The third step is to begin developing the strategy for the attack – this based on knowledge of potential weaknesses or known vulnerabilities. The attacker may select tools to be used in the attack – siege engines, battering rams, catapults and personnel, for example.

Enumeration is the documenting of the system characteristics, which include operating system patch levels, applications running on the system, configurations, user accounts, and any other information that may be strategically important as the attack is planned.

Penetration

The final phase of the attack on the city is the attack itself. During this phase, the attacker will try to exploit the vulnerabilities that were identified and use the tools available to gain access to the city.

Using a variety of tools and techniques, the pen tester will attempt to gain access to the organization's systems. The attack may be based on a tool, social engineering, or physical security attacks. The pen tester must be creative, methodical, flexible and persistent in order to complete a worthwhile test.

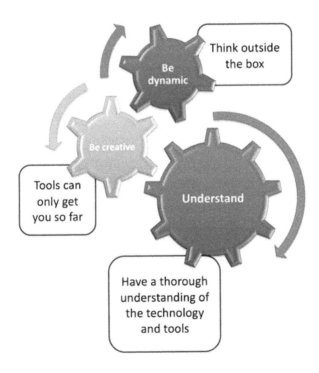

Figure 5: The many facets of pen testing

Once the pen tester has successfully managed to gain access to the system, they will often stop the attack. There is a significant danger that a penetration test will cause system outages and interrupt business operations, so the pen tester must always be careful, be watchful of the ongoing status of the tests, and be ready to work with system administrators to recover the systems if a failure does occur.

Penetration testing versus hacking

The discipline of penetration testing is not to be confused with unethical hacking. A penetration test is an authorized, carefully managed and structured analysis of the security of a system or network, and is done to support the organization that requests it. An unethical hack is an attack against a government, military, corporation or individual that is not authorized by the victim, and may be done with malicious intent. Many individuals and groups (including protestors, criminal organizations, script kiddies, and unethical computer specialists) participate in hacking for various reasons, ranging from financial gain, competitive advantage and military strategy, to revenge, ideology and ego.

The purpose of a penetration test is to simulate the type of attack that an unethical hacker would conduct in order to determine if the client is vulnerable to a hacking attack. The pen tester, therefore, will use many of the same tools and techniques used by an unauthorized attacker. The pen tester must, however, be careful to act within the authorized bounds of the test and respect the privacy and integrity of the client.

Many hackers are brilliant and determined to be successful; they may be very well educated, and supported with the latest tools and equipment. Therefore, the pen tester must realize the seriousness of their work. The pen tester must be thorough and always keep up with an ever-changing threat environment.

Benefits of penetration testing

Conducting a penetration test may provide many benefits for an organization. These may be immediate financial savings in insurance or liability costs, or long term benefits – such as avoiding costly downtime or damage to the reputation of the organization.

In the past few years, major breaches of organizations, such as TJX and the US Department of Veterans Affairs, have cost those organizations in the hundreds of millions of dollars – money that could have been saved and put to much better use if the organizations had been aware of the vulnerabilities that they had. In both the above cases, the attacks would have been easily avoided by way of a few simple changes.

Some of the key benefits of penetration testing include:

- Preservation of customer loyalty
- Better vulnerability management
- A robust security program
- Avoidance of downtime costs
- Meeting of regulatory compliance requirements
- Protection of corporate image and reputation
- Justification of security measures
- Fulfilment of audit requirements.

Summary

Throughout this book, we will look at risk management, threat and vulnerability identification, and detail the steps to take to conduct a penetration test. We will examine the use of some of the most popular and effective tools available today and examine how to conduct an attack against various types of systems, applications and networks. This effort will build towards a successful penetration test and deliver a beneficial result for the client.

Key learning points

The key learning points from this chapter are:

- A penetration test is a business-oriented activity: it must never be conducted without first obtaining the approval of the organization, determining the scope, clarifying the reporting requirements, and selecting the penetration testing techniques, schedule, and plan.
- A penetration test is not simply the use of tools and is more than a technical operation.
- A penetration test must be thorough and executed with skill and discipline.
- A penetration test is conducted through a series of steps that help ensure a successful result.

Questions

1. What is the purpose of a penetration test?
   a) To exploit network vulnerabilities
   b) To provide a report to management on the effectiveness of their security program
   c) To test the effectiveness of a security control
   d) To measure the level of risk to an organization.

Answer: B

Answers A, C, and D are some of the results of the tests, but the main purpose of a test is to support the governance and better management of information systems.

2. Who should conduct a penetration test?
   a) Skilled, authorized professionals
   b) Information technology staff
   c) Outsiders with a love for hacking
   d) Internal staff with an interest in security.

Answer: A

The other answers are not correct, since a penetration test conducted by unskilled, unethical or unauthorized persons can result in serious damage to the organization.

3. What is the first step in a penetration test?
   a) Probing any potential vulnerabilities
   b) Exploiting system flaws or misconfigurations
   c) Gathering data about the client
   d) Reporting on potential vulnerabilities to management.

Answer: C

This is the first step. The other steps will come later in the testing sequence.

4. A penetration testing report should be presented to:
   a) The management team of the organization
   b) IT staff and management only
   c) Authorized personnel only
   d) All staff.

Answer: C

A penetration test is a confidential report that may list serious potential vulnerabilities; it should only be given to authorized personnel.

5. A penetration test is the examination of:
   a) Technical controls
   b) Vulnerabilities in software
   c) Gaps in user training
   d) All controls related to information systems.

Answer: D

The penetration test is the examination of all types of controls within the authorized scope of the test.

CHAPTER 2: PREPARING TO CONDUCT A PENETRATION TEST

Conducting a successful penetration test is a challenge for even the most experienced penetration tester. A penetration test requires perseverance and creativity, as well as a bit of luck. Luck must be earned, however; as Samuel Goldwyn once said, "I make my own luck and the harder I work, the luckier I get.[10]" The pen tester is always best following a clear and structured methodology that will ensure that all possible avenues of attack are explored and no potential vulnerability is overlooked.

Most pen testers use Linux®-based operating systems for their work. A further explanation of Linux, and some if its features can be found in *Appendix 1: Linux,* at the end of this book. A person that is not familiar with Linux may want to read through that appendix before continuing with this chapter.

Approval and scope

The first step in any penetration test must be to obtain formal approval from the business to conduct the test. A penetration test is a risk-filled operation, and the pen tester will want to be protected from any problems that may arise as a result of the test. The penetration test must also be conducted under strict terms of confidentiality and non-disclosure. A penetration tester may learn about serious vulnerabilities in a target network and must never exploit

---

[10] *www.brainyquotes.com.*

those vulnerabilities for any purpose, save the execution of the test. The pen tester must be careful not to disclose the nature of any vulnerability to any unauthorized party, and be careful not to expose any details of the test through conversation, careless handling of test results or end-of-test reports.

The pen tester must also be aware of any legal restrictions related to conducting a pen test or the use of hacking tools. In some countries, the very possession of many tools used in pen testing may be illegal.

Once approval has been granted by senior management to conduct the pen test (often called a "get out of jail free" card), the pen tester will be ready to begin the preparation work leading up to the test itself.

Performing a penetration test is much more than just running some tools or probing some systems. A pen test is a scientific and methodical series of steps and tasks focused on discovering the vulnerabilities in networks, systems, implementations, physical infrastructure, utilities, hardware, user training, procedures and applications.

The first challenge the pen tester faces is to work within the limited amount of information that was provided by the client. There are several types of pen tests – ranging from *blind*, *double blind* and *zero knowledge* to *partial knowledge* and *full knowledge* tests. Each type of test has both advantages and disadvantages.

Internal versus external

The CNSSI 4009 Glossary[11] defines penetration testing as: "Security testing in which evaluators attempt to circumvent the security features of a system based on their understanding of the system design and implementation."

The Information Systems Audit and Control Association (ISACA[12]) defines penetration testing as: "A live test of the effectiveness of security defenses through mimicking the actions of real-life attackers."

We can see from these definitions that penetration testing is not a term restricted to internal or external parties, but can be, and should be, conducted by internal teams where possible, but also by external experts on a regular basis. External teams may provide a level of expertise not available internally and are often more objective or independent in their perspective. This allows them to examine, assess and report on any findings with less of the influence or bias that may curtail the work of an internal team.

Zero knowledge test

A zero knowledge test is conducted by an external party that is provided a bare minimum of information to work from. These tests are not as common as partial knowledge tests and may be the most challenging and difficult for the pen testing team. The first step is to learn as much about the client as possible from public sources or social engineering.

---

[11] *CNSSI 4009: National Information Assurance Glossary* (2003), www.cnss.gov/Assets/pdf/cnssi_4009.pdf.
[12] www.isaca.org.

This type of test most closely resembles the type of attack performed by an attacker that does not have inside knowledge of the target and must seek out the information that is available through searches and probes of publicly available data.

There are numerous examples of organizations that have benefitted from a zero knowledge test through discovering that a great deal of sensitive information about their organization was available in publicly accessible places. In two cases involving large and highly sensitive organizations, the testers found application source code that was being posted by developers onto user groups for the purpose of getting help from other programmers to solve application-coding challenges. Such a breach could provide an attacker with a considerable advantage in planning an attack.

Partial knowledge test

In a partial knowledge test, the testing team is provided some degree of detail about systems, IP addresses, network configurations, physical locations, or any other such details the client decides to provide. The partial knowledge test is the most common type of test conducted by external parties and is often the most economical and effective. The testing team can quickly target the focus of the test and quickly assess the security of the system.

Full knowledge test

A full knowledge test is usually only conducted by an internal testing team that has complete access to system and network configurations. These tests are often conducted on a regular (perhaps even continuous) basis, as the organization monitors and examines their own network controls and ability to withstand an attack.

Blind test

One of the primary benefits of a penetration test is the opportunity to assess the watchfulness and response of the network and systems administrators. In a blind test, the test is conducted without the knowledge of the administrators. The testing team will watch to see if the test is detected by the administrators and, if it is, they will observe their reaction to it. This allows management to refine the processes used to monitor and respond to network attacks, as well as to assess the robustness of the controls. Some organizations provide incentives to reward administrators if they do notice the attack, either while it is ongoing, or if they detect the evidence of the attack through examining the logs following the attack.

Double blind test

A double blind attack is conducted in the same manner as a blind attack, except that, in the case of a double blind attack, neither the security team or the administrators are informed of the attack. Again, this allows the testing team to advise management on the ability of the organization to detect and respond appropriately to an attack.

Planning

A penetration test is a methodical and very carefully planned activity that must be conducted in an organized and well-managed manner. Planning for the test will include team selection, obtaining access and preparing to conduct the test.

Team selection

The pen testing team must be carefully screened to ensure that they are suitably trained and that they will not abuse the privileges or access that they will have. They must also agree not to disclose or use any of the knowledge they gain in doing the penetration test to the detriment of the client. This requires the signing of non-disclosure agreements and may require the testing team to be subjected to background checks to ensure that they do not have a criminal or an undesirable background. If a company chooses to engage an individual with an undesirable background, and that individual goes on to commit an improper act during or following the test, then company may find itself in a difficult legal position.

The skills needed to be an excellent penetration tester include a broad understanding of systems, networks and business functions. The tester should be good at communicating with the various members of the organization – including management, users and administrators – and proficient at writing and presenting reports on the results of their tests. It must be remembered that the purpose of a test is to help secure the business and allow the business to operate in a reliable manner, even though it is operating in a dangerous world that is full of risk. A report containing recommendations that would disable the systems of the organization and would result in the inability to conduct business would not be acceptable and only lead to the loss of credibility of the testing team. It may result in the rejection of their other recommendations, as well.

No single person is capable of performing all parts of a broad penetration test equally well, so it may be necessary to select team members that have varied areas of expertise. Some people are much better at social engineering or physical security testing, while others are experts in testing UNIX®-based systems or focusing on a Windows®-based network.

Access

Gaining access to systems is an important part of the test planning process. In many cases, an external testing team will want to place someone inside the organization, who can monitor the test and enable the testing team to react quickly if the test affects production systems or impacts business operations. This requires setting up access, allocating workspace and, possibly, arranging some level of network and communications access.

The test should be conducted in conditions that resemble the real world as much as possible. Some testing teams have asked the client organization to open certain firewall ports or enable certain services in order to conduct the test. This adjustment would mean, however, that the testing team would conduct the test in a world somewhat different from that which a hacker would encounter if trying to break in; and this would devalue the results of the test. A good pen testing team should be able to conduct the test without requiring changes being made to the organization's networks or security controls.

Tools

Throughout this book, we will be looking at some of the tools used by a testing team. These tools are powerful and may be very damaging to client systems or business processes. Therefore, they must be used carefully and steps must be taken to ensure that the testers are both familiar with and know the risks associated with each of them.

A good tester will know how to use a variety of tools and techniques to conduct a test, and will be able to tune their attacks in order to adjust to the conditions and challenges found during it.

The selection of tools to be used during the test should be based on the type of testing being conducted. For example, it may be necessary to be discreet or conduct the test in a discreet manner, or the test may involve being quite noisy and aggressive.

Rules of engagement

Both before the test commences and during the signing of the testing agreement, the rules of engagement for the test should be documented. These will cover what the team should, or should not, be allowed to do (such as social engineering, gaining physical access, creating fake files, gaining elevated access, etc.) The testing team must know what to do if they gain access and know when to cease the test if there is a risk of compromise of the operations or confidentiality of the business.

Reporting

The final part of the pen test is the delivering of the report detailing the results of the test to management. The contract should already have confirmed whom the report will be provided to and the level of detail and content required. It should also state the obligation of the testing team to keep the report confidential and to not discuss the results of the test with unauthorized personnel.

Contracts

A pen test should only be conducted under the terms of a contract that stipulates the scope, responsibilities, authority and conditions under which the test is to be conducted. All of the details provided earlier, such as those about confidentiality, reporting, non-disclosure, permission for access, scope, the rules of engagement and the team member selection criteria should be addressed in the contract.

Scope

Rarely can an organization do one test that will test the entire organization, so the scope must be determined in advance of the test and documented in the contract. The scope may be limited to only web-facing systems, or it may include physical pen testing or social engineering; it may look only at UNIX systems or the Windows®-based network, or it may be based in one geographic region of operations or focused on one department, product or service. In some cases, such as PCI DSS compliance, the scope and frequency of the tests may be mandated by regulation, standards or corporate policy.

An organization should conduct various types of tests of varying scope or focus, so that all parts of the organization will eventually be examined.

Liability

An important part of any agreement to conduct a pen test should be the consideration of liability. The organization requesting the test must be aware of the risks associated with the test. They must also be aware of the risks of damaging the client organization, improper disclosure of confidential client data and the risk of violating laws of a country that the organization is operating in. In some countries, the very possession of tools used for conducting a pen test may be illegal.

The contracts between the organization requesting the test and the testing team should address the risk of liability and non-performance, and each organization should have insurance coverage to protect themselves from undue loss or hardship.

In the case of any disagreement between the parties involved, the contract should also address the jurisdiction for hearing any complaints or engaging other legal proceedings.

Summary

A pen test is a carefully planned and managed task that requires contractual agreements, governance and oversight, and a prior agreement on the conditions, reporting and methods to be used in conducting the test.

Questions

1. A penetration test is:
   a) Innovative and unmanaged
   b) Creative and well-controlled
   c) Carefully structured and restrictive
   d) Disorganized and reactive.

Answer: B

A pen test must be carefully managed and controlled. It should also be innovative and carefully structured, but it should not be disorganized, unmanaged or reactive. The test may be restrictive, depending on the environment, but B is a better answer than C.

2. A pen testing contract should cover:
   a) Non-disclosure agreements
   b) Which client staff are to be interviewed
   c) A list of tools to be used
   d) The transfer of liability to the testing organization.

Answer: A

A pen testing contract should cover non-disclosure agreements, scope, reporting requirements, authority and rules of engagement, but will not require the listing of tools, selection of individuals or the transfer of liability. Instead, it should list the criteria for testing conditions and the assumption of liability.

3. A blind test is where:
   a) The security team is not informed about the test
   b) The testing team is not provided any information about the client systems
   c) The systems and network administrators of the client organization are not informed of the test
   d) The tools to be used in the test will not disclose any confidential or sensitive information about the client systems the testing team.

Answer: C

This is the definition of a blind test. A double blind test would not disclose the details to the security team.

4. A pen test should be performed as directed by:
   a) The policy of the organization
   b) Industry standards
   c) Risk management teams
   d) The amount of change to business and IT processes.

Answer: A

All of the other answers may influence the decision on when to conduct a pen test, but the pen test should only be scheduled when it is in accordance with the policy of the organization and senior management direction.

5. The pen tester notices a potential vulnerability that is on a system outside of the scope of the test. What should the pen tester do?
   a) Do more testing to validate whether the vulnerability is real
   b) Ignore the vulnerability, since it is out of scope
   c) Download the patch to fix the vulnerability
   d) Report the existence of the vulnerability to management.

Answer: D

The correct action is to report the situation. The pen tester should never undertake any activity outside of the scope of the authorized test.

CHAPTER 3: RECONNAISSANCE

The start of the test

Now that the preparatory work has been completed and the testing team knows the scope, authority and rules of engagement for the test, the real pen testing work begins. The first step in conducting a pen test is to get to know the target. The test requires knowledge of client networks, applications, physical facilities, equipment and the people that use, manage and oversee client systems. It must be remembered that a pen test is often much more than just a technical probe of a system or technology. The test may be multifaceted and also examine physical, procedural and administrative controls.

The pen tester will use several methods to gather information about the target organization. These information-gathering techniques will include the same types of steps taken by an attacker attempting to probe the systems of networks of a potential victim.

Physical information gathering

Physical information gathering includes several techniques, including gaining physical access and the various types of social engineering.

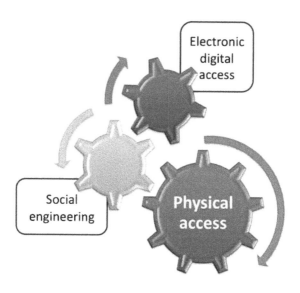

Figure 6: Data gathering sources

Physical access

The pen tester will often test the physical access controls of the organization by methods such as attempting to bypass security procedures, defeating locks, and using alternative manners of entry (including roof access, loading docks and other access points). Of course, it is important to make sure that proper authorization is obtained before attempting such tests and that there is no physical risk to the tester.

Figure 7: Physical penetration testing

It can accurately be stated that breaches of physical security can have more impact than a breach of any other security control. If an attacker can gain physical access to systems, equipment, equipment rooms, network cables and personnel, then they can successfully execute virtually any type of attack and gain nearly unlimited access to data or sensitive information.

Social engineering

Social engineering is the manipulation of people to convince them to provide information or access that should not have been granted to the attacker (the engineer). This is one of the most common methods used to gain access to an organization or to gather sensitive data, and is very often successful. Social engineering takes many forms, including intimidation, name-dropping, appealing for assistance, and technical attacks.

Intimidation: This is the coercion or threatening of a victimized employee that causes the victim to provide access or information. This may work if the culture of the organization discourages employees from challenging a person that appears to be in authority. In the past, the intimidation method has been carried out successfully to gain access to military locations – if an attacker is dressed in the uniform of a senior officer, the guards may be afraid to challenge the imposter and allow the "officer" to gain unauthorized access. Some senior managers may also use intimidating behavior to pressure subordinates or other staff to break the rules and permit co-workers, visitors or other personnel to perform tasks that they should not have been permitted to do.

Name-dropping: This is one of the most common attacks. The attacker convinces the victim that the attacker has the approval from a person in authority to perform a restricted function or have access to protected data. The attacker may learn the name of the person in authority from a public source (such as an annual report or press release) and tell the victim that "Mr Davies," for example, has granted them permission to gain access to the data or system in question.

Appealing for assistance: This is an attack that takes advantage of the helpful and good nature of people that would like to provide assistance to a person in need. The attacker asks the victim to help them solve a problem they are having – such as having trouble gaining remote access. The helpful victim may offer to help them use their account for access or set up an alternative way for the attacker to get the access or information they need.

Technical attacks: These are very common these days and take many forms. Many technical attacks come in the form of e-mails that promise jobs, lottery winnings, loans or other incentives. The attacker convinces the victim to disclose personal information that can then be used by the attacker to exploit the victim or the victim's organization. The attack on RSA was facilitated by an employee opening an e-mail attachment that purported to list job opportunities.

Dumpster diving

Dumpster diving – going through the trash, garbage and recycling bins of an organization – is also a form of social engineering. The method is to simply sift through the discarded papers of an organization, looking for confidential data or technical manuals that may contain information that could aid an attacker in launching an attack. Many organizations have unknowingly provided the information needed to break into their systems by discarding old manuals that may have had passwords written in the notes and details on how to configure or connect to systems.

The pen tester will often use forms of social engineering to test the defenses and controls of the organization. One test has been to leave USB sticks lying around a facility and hope that staff will find them and take them into the office with them. The USB sticks may contain a Trojan horse or other malware that can then be used to gain access to the corporate network.

These attacks show that the secret to a successful pen test may be to attack the organization via its own personnel – this is often a very successful attack angle.

As will be seen later in this book, the pen tester must report on the success of such attacks and can then recommend steps that can be taken to mitigate them – often through improved awareness training.

Publicly available information

The first step in data gathering is to research publicly available data sources for information about the target company. Most companies have vast amounts of information available via the Internet, which can disclose potential attack vectors and enable social engineering or technical attacks to succeed. There are several examples of companies that have found source code for their applications posted on the Internet in user groups or chat rooms in which the company's developers were searching for advice on solving programming problems. It is not uncommon to find that employees have been posting articles and comments on weblogs (blogs) that may indicate the types of equipment and other practices in use at the organization. Employee e-mail addresses, user IDs and passwords may also be freely available.

Social engineering and data mining in publicly available data are the least technical of all the steps in a penetration test. Anybody can do extensive searches on an organization. Most people are familiar with the tools and search engines that can be used – search engines, such as Google, Yahoo! and Bing, provide an easy way to discover information that the organization may not realize is commonly available. It is not uncommon to find passwords, conference presentations, or information about systems, equipment or personnel readily available using search engines. Many web archives also contain information about organizations and individuals that may make the attacker's job easier. Archived web pages may also be available on the Wayback Machine.

Wireless penetration

Wireless devices provide a great benefit to an organization due to their greater mobility and easier access, but, as is well known, they can also provide access for an attacker. Wireless devices may be easily accessible from outside the building and allow an attacker to gain access to internal networks without even stepping onto the property of the victim organization. Thinking to "hide" wireless access points by turning off the service set identifier (SSID) broadcast or using Media Access Control (MAC) filtering is an ineffective control. A pen tester should look for authorized and unauthorized wireless devices during a test. The breach of T.J.Maxx in the United States, which led to the compromise of over 49 million credit cards, was enabled through an authorized, but insecure, wireless access point. Since many laptops have Bluetooth,® IEEE 802.11 and USB mobile access, it is relatively easy to find unsecured wireless channels into the networks and systems of the target organization that are located behind firewalls.

Other data sources

There are many other sources of information that can be used in the data gathering stage of a pen test. These include social networking sites, instant messages and blogs.

Social networking sites

It may be surprising to see how much information is willingly provided every day by users of social networking sites. Employees of organizations share information about their lives, work and relationships that may give an attacker an opportunity to build relationships with them that may then be leveraged to obtain competitive information or access to the strategies of the organization. Posting organizational information may also lead to the loss of ownership of that information. This may be a risk when an organization wants to promote a marketing plan without realizing that doing this may allow another organization to use that information without penalty.

Instant messaging and blogs

Anything posted in an instant messaging (IM) system or a blog must be considered public information. Organizational policy should direct how employees use instant messaging or participate in blogs. This policy should include a directive that no corporate data or files be shared using instant messaging. In some countries, the use of IM to communicate with customers would be a matter of official record and all IM traffic must be stored for a period of seven or more years.

It has not been uncommon to find that developers and other staff have contributed to internet forums and blogs that will reveal information about their organization – including source code and equipment configurations at times.

Domain name system (DNS)

The domain name system is a crucial part of the Internet, and using fully qualified domain names (FQDNs) – instead of using IP addresses – provides an easy way for most people to reach web pages. When registering their domain name with the DNS, the organization is required to provide some publicly available information, such as phone numbers, addresses and the names of administrators when they register their domain name. This information may then be used in social engineering attacks. The pen tester will look up the DNS registration as a part of data gathering.

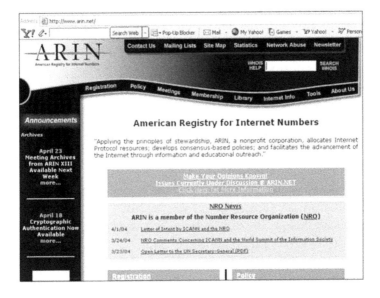

Figure 8: DNS listing

Banner grabbing

Banner grabbing is the act of reviewing the metadata banner that is a header in the communications channel that is set up between the two remote entities. By reviewing the banner, the pen tester can often learn information about the operating system and other services running on the target machine.

Footprinting

Through both active and passive reconnaissance, the pen tester can learn a lot about the target's networks, system layout, configurations and patch levels.

While passive reconnaissance is the quiet method of gathering information without contacting the target systems and trying to go as unnoticed as possible, active reconnaissance is the probing and prodding of the target systems and networks. The tester learns about the target through the ways that the systems respond to queries or react to probes.

The purpose of footprinting is to gather as much information about the target as possible, so that the pen tester can design the subsequent pen tests to exactly target the discovered vulnerabilities and be successful. The footprint of the system should include a diagram of the target network and a description of system services, equipment and patch levels.

The use of products, such as Maltego and FireCAT, will help the pen tester map out the networks and the relationships between data, systems and services. Refined Google searches will also present a wealth of information to the tester.

Job postings

The pen tester may also review job postings that have been posted on public areas, since they will often describe the qualifications and experience needed by a job applicant. The posting will often disclose the types of equipment, software and methodologies used by the target organization.

Reviewing Securities and Exchange Commission (SEC) filings for publicly traded companies or other publicly available information, such as company listings, search results of executive staff in people search engines and comments in news media will often uncover extensive information that may be valuable to the pen tester.

Traceroute

A very useful tool for the pen tester is *traceroute*. Traceroute will identify the path taken by traffic travelling to the target network. It will allow the pen tester to learn some of the behaviors of the traffic using of Time to Live (TTL) statistics and response times. This can assist the pen tester in determining the presence and layout of various network devices.

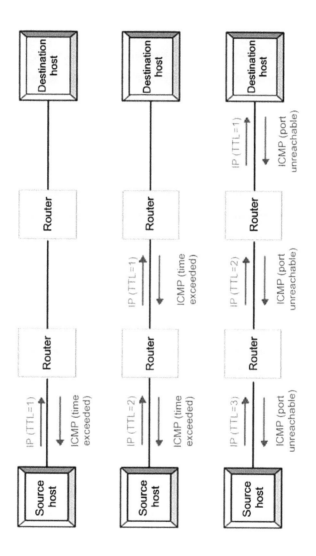

Figure 9: Traceroute

Avoiding footprinting

An organization that wants to minimize the impact of footprinting needs to be careful what information is available publicly about the company. This may require the sanitizing of DNS registries, the careful wording of job postings and clear policies for staff that review or contribute to blogs or other interactive forums. The organization should also have separate internal and external DNS servers, since an attacker may learn network configuration information from the internal DNS.

DNS zone transfers

In order to replicate the data stored on a DNS server, an administrator can perform a *zone transfer*. The problem is that an attacker can also copy the DNS data in the same manner. If the DNS server is on the internal network, this would allow the attacker to learn information that may assist in the execution of an attack. Attackers also can successfully poison DNS entries, so that requests to a website are diverted to an alternate location.

Key learning points

There is a wealth of information publicly available about most organizations, and the pen tester should take the time to uncover as much of it as possible. This will enable a targeted test, which is much more likely to be successful and may avoid a lot of wasted time and effort later in the pen testing process.

Footprinting is a combination of technical, social and physical tests – some of which are passive in nature and some of which are active.

Every organization should take steps to minimize the amount of information publicly available about their systems, networks, software, processes and staff.

Questions

1. The purpose of footprinting is to:
   a) Test of the ability of the systems administrators to detect and respond to a penetration
   b) Review and audit whether the administrators are complying with organizational procedures
   c) Detect any misconfigurations of network or host equipment
   d) Gather information about a target organization.

Answer: D

2. Social engineering can be described as:
   a) Aggressively marketing the organization through social media
   b) Managing the social perception of the organization through press releases and media manipulation
   c) Influencing a person to provide access or information against the policies of the organization
   d) The engineering and design of systems through a committee-based approach.

Answer: C

3. Google hacking is:
   a) Exploiting weaknesses in the security infrastructure of Google
   b) Using Google tools to hack into an organization
   c) The discovery of information about an organization using Google features
   d) The footprinting of the Google network layout and international server relationships.

Answer: C

4. Traceroute is used to:
   a) Discover the path taken by packets across a network
   b) Determine response times for database queries
   c) Track the activity on a network and monitor error levels
   d) Evaluate whether the Time to Live (TTL) is set properly for internal network communications.

Answer: A

5. With regards to DNS servers, the organization should:
   a) Ensure they contain as much information as possible to speed up network traffic
   b) Always have separate internal and external DNS servers to provide better efficiency
   c) Deploy separate internal and external DNS servers to hide internal network data from external parties
   d) Configure DNS servers to point to authoritative domain hosts.

Answer: C

CHAPTER 4: ACTIVE RECONNAISSANCE AND ENUMERATION

Active reconnaissance is the next critical step in the pen testing process. During this step, the pen tester will learn crucial information about the characteristics of the target system (and perhaps even about the administrators' diligence in monitoring, patching and configuring the systems properly).

Active reconnaissance is the actual probing of the system to learn how it is configured, what possible points of entry there are for the pen tester and what services or vulnerable points may be found.

Active reconnaissance may consist of several types of tests, including port scans, operating system fingerprinting, and Transmission Control Protocol (TCP) scanning. It can be compared to knocking on every door in a hotel or apartment building to see which rooms are in use, which doors are locked, and which rooms issue a response.

Closely linked with active reconnaissance is enumeration. Enumeration is the retrieval of specific information about the target systems, user accounts and passwords that may identify vulnerabilities and attack vectors that can be used by the pen tester – or an attacker – in a subsequent attack.

Through the process of enumeration, the objective is to gather as much information as possible about network resources, usernames, passwords, active services and machine names.

Port scanning

Network communications and applications are set to transfer information over predefined ports. These ports are similar to the rooms in a hotel – some rooms are occupied and in use, while others are vacant. A thief wanting to gain access to valuables that residents of the hotel may have in their rooms will not want to waste time entering rooms that are not in use. Therefore, the thief may first listen at the door (passive reconnaissance) and then perhaps even knock on the door to see if anyone answers (active reconnaissance). The purpose of port scanning is to see which doors or ports are open on a system, so that the pen tester can target their attack to the services, ports and applications that are in use.

Applications are usually related to certain ports, such as port 25 for SMTP (e-mail), port 80 for web applications, port 443 for Secure Sockets Layer (SSL), and port 53 for DNS. Any open port is a target and opportunity for an attacker, so those that are not needed should be closed. The less attack surface area the organization has, the easier it is to defend. Every open door requires that much more work to protect and monitor.

A port scan sends a request to each port to see if it will respond. If it does, it may be possible for the tester to learn information, such as the operating system in use and the services available, and, from that information, begin to draw out a network blueprint.

It is important to note that a port scan is nothing more than a knock on a door and is not illegal in most cases – but the pen tester must know the laws and regulations for the country they are operating in. Some countries may consider a port scan to be a demonstration of intent to break in and, therefore, unlawful.

The first step in port scanning is often to use the Internet Control Message Protocol (ICMP) to ping the target network. Hosts on a network that allow pings will respond to the pings, thereby revealing their presence. Open source tools like Nmap® are frequently used for this type of test. Nmap can then also be used to do more thorough tests without using the ping feature. In this way, Nessus is used for operating system fingerprinting and patch level detection.

The use of the three-way handshake of TCP is also a way to determine which ports are open on a system. A TCP-connect port scan will attempt to sequentially connect to each port on a system. If a port is open, then the target port should respond to a SYN request with a SYN/ACK; otherwise, it will respond with a RST/ACK or no reply (if filtered). Many systems are filtered, which means that responses to a scan may be blocked.

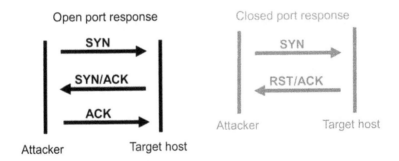

Figure 10: TCP scanning

The tester may also choose to do a half-open TCP SYN port scan instead of a TCP-connect scan. In this case, the third part of the TCP three-way handshake is not completed. This method is commonly used when an attacker wants to conduct a distributed denial-of-service (DDoS) attack against a victim by sending a flood of SYN packets towards the victim and never responding to the SYN/ACK that the victim sends back.

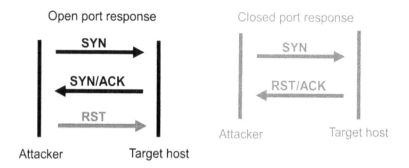

Figure 11: TCP half-open scan

User Datagram Protocol (UDP) scans may also be used to detect open or closed ports. A UDP message is sent to the target system and the tester will note whether the system responds with a "port unreachable" reply, indicating a closed port.

Nmap can be used to do UDP scans by using the -aU argument.

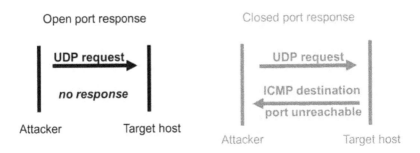

Figure 12: UDP scan

Adding additional conditions to an Nmap test will provide more data about the target operating system, and allow the pen tester to adjust their attacks accordingly. However, some Nmap tests can be very noisy and are more likely to attract the attention of the target system and intrusion detection system (IDS).

Other common tools used for scanning include hping2, SuperScan® and Look@LAN.

Web server banners

Learning what type of equipment and operating systems are being used by a web server will provide a strategic advantage to the attacker. Such information is readily available from many servers through simple actions. Establishing a telnet session to the web server by typing "telnet <webserver> 80" and then the command "GET / HTTP/1.0" works on many older systems; and the use of tools, such as SuperScan and HTTPRINT, are effective against some newer systems. Establishing a telnet session to a SMTP server over port 25 can also disclose the software version that is being used by the SMTP server.

> To establish a telnet session:
> 1. From a command prompt, type in "telnet <IP> 80"
> 2. Type in "Head/HTTP 1.0"
> 3. Press "Enter" or "Return" twice.

```
C:\WINDOWS\system32\cmd.exe

HTTP/1.1 200 OK
Content-Length: 1433
Content-Type: text/html
Content-Location: http://192.168.1.10/iisstart.htm
Last-Modified: Fri, 21 Feb 2003 18:48:30 GMT
Accept-Ranges: bytes
ETag: "0938ad3d9d9c21:33a"
Server: Microsoft-IIS/6.0
X-Powered-By: ASP.NET
Date: Sat, 22 Oct 2005 23:15:43 GMT
Connection: close
```

Figure 13: Web banner grabbing using telnet

SuperScan can also be used for Web Banner Grabbing, as seen below.

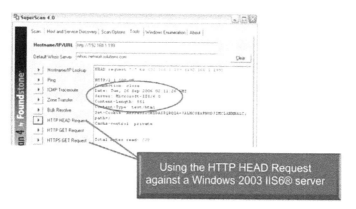

Figure 14: Banner grabbing using SuperScan

DNS vulnerabilities

The tools nslookup and BackTrack® are the attacker's and pen tester's friends when it comes to enumerating the characteristics of the DNS configurations. Zone transfers and data about server names and addresses can be queried from any DNS attached to the Internet. This is why it is important to always have separate internal and external DNS servers, and to ensure that they are configured correctly to prevent zone transfers.

Simple Network Management Protocol (SNMP®) insecurity

SNMP is a very useful tool for network and system administrators; however, the earlier versions – SNMPv1 and SNMPv2 – are not secure enough for use. These versions pass the community string (the password, if you will) in cleartext and the default setting of "public" is often still set. The community string should be set to a cryptic value and ports 161 and 162 should be blocked at the firewall.

Administrators should use SNMPv3 wherever possible. Where older equipment does not support this version, however, the SNMP traffic can be encrypted over Internet Protocol Security (IPsec), or all SNMP connections can be restricted to respond to predefined IP addresses only.

Active Directory® enumeration

Active Directory (AD) will contain the user names and access rights for all the users on a system. Learning user names will provide the attacker with a great advantage in targeting an attack – especially as some names may indicate job roles and obviously be set for high-level access. Lightweight Directory Access Protocol (LDAP) is used to access AD following the X.500 naming standards. LdapMiner is a tool that can be used to search AD entries. Administrators should also consider blocking ports 389 (LDAP) and 3268 (global catalog) at the firewall.

Null sessions

If an attacker/pen tester can establish a null session to a server, a whole list of new attacks and the use of many more tools – such as Cain & Abel, DumpSec and THC-Hydra – will be possible. These tools gather network and user information, allow the attacker to establish new user accounts and grab password hashes. The best countermeasures to this are to disable ports that may not be needed, such as port 135 (Remote Procedure Call (RPC) locator); 137 (Windows® Internet Name Service (WINS)); 138 (Network Basic Input/Output System (NetBIOS®)); and 445 (Common Internet File System / Server Message Block (CIFS/SMB)).

Countermeasures to active reconnaissance

Organizations should harden their systems by turning off services and ports that are not needed. Every port is a possible point of attack, and a breach at any point in the network may lead to a compromise in other locations.

The corporate firewall is the first layer of defense and should be configured to block inbound ICMP packets, detect and drop any abnormal packets and monitor all network connections.

The intrusion detection system (IDS) should also be set to detect port scans and terminate the connections.

A layered defense is the secret to true security. Just as in a hotel, where valuables are locked in a safe in the room, on a network the ports should be closed, the IDS enabled, the application level monitoring in use and proxies used to hide network information.

Perhaps the most important countermeasure to an attack is to monitor system activity and check system logs frequently. Many times, the administrator may become aware of a probing attack from a remote entity through evidence in the logs. While it may be impossible to stop an attacker from probing and attempting to break in, by knowing about the malicious activity, the administrator can take steps to block the amount of information available or to block the access ports open to the attacker.

Key learning points

Active reconnaissance is one of the most important steps in a penetration test. It enables the tester to learn about the actual configurations and potential technical weaknesses of the system, and thereby prepare test scenarios targeted specifically at those vulnerable points. Port scans, TCP-connect and TCP half-open scans are some of the most popular methods of scanning. Many attacks are enabled by administrators leaving ports open that may not be needed, or by not enforcing good password rules.

Questions

1. Which of the following would be an example of active reconnaissance?
   a) Eavesdropping on a communications line
   b) Capturing unencrypted wireless traffic to an authorized wireless access point
   c) Scanning well-known ports on a system to determine system responses
   d) Social engineering the administrators to provide unauthorized access to a system.

Answer: C

2. A TCP half-open scan will:
   a) Set up a completed handshake with a target system
   b) Send a series of pings over the target network
   c) Respond with all ports open to a network scan
   d) Send a SYN request to a target, but fail to respond to the subsequent SYN/ACK reply.

Answer: D

3. A ping scan may be illegal if it:
   a) Causes a denial of service on the target network
   b) Responds to a SYN request with a counterattacking RST
   c) Disables the TCP-connect feature on a firewall
   d) Completes a three-way handshake with an infected source system.

Answer: A

4. One reason to use SNMPv3 is:
   a) The earlier versions are too slow to allow for productive remote maintenance
   b) SNMPv1 and SNMPv2 pass the community string in cleartext
   c) SNMPv3 is supported by all versions and generations of equipment
   d) SNMPv1 and SNMPv2 are restricted to internal networks only.

Answer: B

CHAPTER 5: VULNERABILITY ASSESSMENTS

This section is one of the most important areas of concern for the systems, network and database administrators – as well as for the pen tester. Vulnerability assessment is the careful, thorough and diligent review of the target system from all angles and attack vectors. It is through a complete and comprehensive vulnerability assessment (VA) that all the possible means of attack are explored and, from this, the tester will be able to identify all potential attack vectors, potential weaknesses and possible entry points. A pen test without a comprehensive VA is incomplete and will often lead to a false sense of security. The vulnerability assessment will provide invaluable information for the administrators as well. This will assure them of whether there are previously unknown or unidentified holes in their security infrastructure.

Going back to the analogy of a walled medieval city, the pen tester can be seen as the General tasked with planning the attack to take over the city. The General must consider all possible attack angles in estimating the strength of the defenses, determining the best way to attack and deciding which resources are required to launch the attack. The General must walk around the city looking for weak points, examining defensive strategies and considering the best way to proceed. Without proper reconnaissance, the General may attack a point on the city that is well defended and miss the opportunity to attack via a port or gateway that is relatively undefended. A pen tester that only attacks from one angle, or attempts to evaluate a single control, cannot provide assurance to the organization that their infrastructure is adequately protected and that their security controls are robust and effective.

A vulnerability assessment can be defined as the systematic examination of a system to identify areas that may be at risk of an attack. The VA will lead to the evaluation of the effectiveness, completeness and adequacy of the controls, in order to provide the information required by the organization to strengthen their security, plan their security strategy; and by the pen tester to plan the next stage of an penetration-testing attack.

The results of the VA should be a list of potential vulnerabilities with a ranking of the relative risk level for each. Just providing a list of potential vulnerabilities, without providing a list of the relative importance of each vulnerability, can overwhelm an organization with data that is hard for them to sift through, and can make it difficult for the organization to set priorities for addressing the reported vulnerabilities.

The attack vectors

The advantage for a pen tester is that there are many more attack vectors available today than in medieval times. The wall of the city created a defined security perimeter that does not exist in a modern network. A network can be attacked at any level – from a physical to a hardware level, and from communications ports to the whole operating system. In addition, the application itself can be attacked directly through the network and any vulnerabilities in the application can overcome all the other network defenses in place. The problem is that most pen testers forget to assess all the vulnerabilities when they conduct a pen test – they focus on technical issues and web applications, overlooking the many other avenues of attack that could be exploited. Many amateur hackers make the same mistake, but professional attackers and advanced persistent threats (APTs) will test every possible attack angle until they discover an open vulnerability or attack vector.

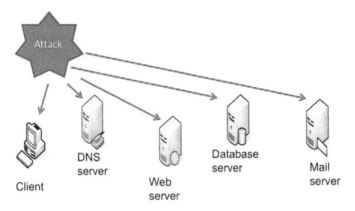

Figure 15: Attack (and test) vectors

A medieval city could usually only be attacked on one plane – the ground or, perhaps, a tunnel under the ground – but a network must be defended at every level, every angle, and in such a way as to not only protect against external threats, but also against internally-based threats or misuse.

Estimates claim that 48-70% of all successful attacks were made possible through an internal factor, such as a misconfiguration, social engineering or employee malfeasance. The pen tester should watch for such vulnerabilities and ensure that the organization is protected from internal threats, as well as external attacks.

Testing for the effectiveness of a security control often consists of three levels of evaluation. The first involves ensuring that the control was indeed implemented as designed. There can often be a mismatch between design and implementation, and this may lead to an undocumented gap in the security fabric.

The second level of evaluation involves ensuring that the control is working correctly – in other words, that it is performing the function that it was designed to perform (i.e. a firewall needs to be tested to ensure that it is, in fact, blocking the unwanted traffic, yet allowing authorized traffic).

The third level involves comparing the effectiveness of the control with regard to minimizing risk. Every control is implemented for a reason – and that is to counter a risk. No organization should implement controls that are not needed, nor should they ignore serious risks and not implement the appropriate levels of control. However, a control that was implemented correctly (according to the design) and is operating correctly may still be ineffective if it is not mitigating the risk as was intended by the designer. This is the true art of pen testing. Trust nothing. Test everything. The fact that a front door is locked is of little value if the backdoor is open; a firewall that is working correctly and according to the design is of little use if it is installed in the wrong place. This is where the skill of the pen tester in finding and enumerating every vulnerability (according to the scope of the project, of course) is proven. As it is written in one document, the task is to discover the information protection needs of the organization. "Discover" is a very accurate and appropriate word. Vulnerability assessment is not just about filling in a checklist or running a tool – it is the voyage of discovery and investigation. In many cases, it is discovery; the organization itself does not know its security needs, vulnerabilities and requirements and it is the knowledge and expertise of the pen tester that will reveal these needs to them.

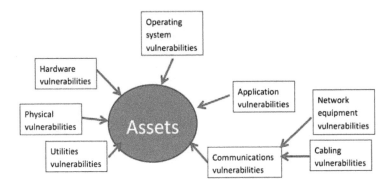

Figure 16: Attack vectors

References and sources of vulnerabilities

There are many good sources available that list known vulnerabilities in equipment, protocols, systems, software and configurations. The pen tester should be familiar with these sources and examine the target systems to ensure that these known vulnerabilities are not present on the system. In most cases, it will be found that known problems still exist on the network, and resolving those issues is the first step in enhancing the overall security of the system. After all, if the presence of a vulnerability is well known to the security community, then it must be assumed that attackers know to look for those weaknesses too.

Some of the sources available to the pen tester and administrator that give information about vulnerabilities include:

Organization	Website
SANS	*www.sans.org*
National Vulnerability Database	*http://nvd.nist.gov*
Common Vulnerabilities and Exposures	*http://cve.mitre.org*
Security Focus	*www.securityfocus.com*
Security Radar	*www.securitywizardry.com/radar.htm*

Figure 17: Sources of information on vulnerabilities

Using vulnerability assessment tools

There are excellent tools available for conducting a vulnerability assessment, and each tool is an important part of the pen tester's arsenal. Most of the tools require practice and further analysis, but they can conduct a wide range of tests in a relatively short time, and provide a very good series of tests against common vulnerability lists and industry-leading resources.

Some of the common tools are:

• Nessus®
• SAINT®
• Retina®
• Qualys.®

Reliance on tools

The pen tester must combine their expertise with the use of tools in order to provide meaningful results. A tool is only as good as the user, and the tool can never replace some of the expertise and creativity of an excellent pen tester. A tool will indicate possible vulnerabilities, but many of the issues found by the tool may be false positives (problems that are indicated, but are not really problems); a tool may also miss some important vulnerabilities – false negatives (problems that exist, but were not identified by the tool). The pen tester must review and examine the results generated by the tool to determine which issues identified by the tool are serious, which are of medium concern, and which issues may be put aside for future review, or ignored altogether.

Patch management

Patch management is a never-ending and challenging task for operations and administration staff. New patches may come out from various vendors at unpredictable times and with varying levels of importance. Some patches are released in an emergency scenario – where a serious exploit of a vulnerability in software may be imminent or already known – while other patches may be less critical and only designed to address performance issues or small glitches in an operational function. The administrator is firstly challenged to roll out the patches to the systems – which, of course, firstly means that the administrator must be aware that a patch has been issued. This administrator must then address both the risk that implementing the patch will affect other business operations and the difficult job of arranging for the systems to be brought down for enough time for the patch to be applied.

Because of these challenges, a vulnerability assessment often finds that the patch levels on systems are not up to date. This situation can pose a very serious risk to the organization.

PCI DSS requirements

For organizations that process payment card data (from credit and debit cards), there are industry standards[13] that must be met to protect cardholder data and prevent the compromise of sensitive information. These standards provide an excellent summary of some of the actions that an organization can take to create a secure operational environment. The standards include the use of a firewall, demilitarized zone (DMZ) and anti-virus product, as well as the regular (quarterly) review of the security of the organization's systems. The quarterly vulnerability assessments are designed to ensure that the organization maintains an adequate security posture.

Malicious code

The test of any network or system should also include a review to see if the organization has been infected with some form of malicious code. There are many forms of malicious code that can infect an organization and be used to open backdoors for an attack, capture passwords or other sensitive information, and damage or destroy system services.

---

[13] *www.pcisecuritystandards.org/.*

Many forms of malicious code spread through e-mail attachments, infected websites or by wrapping themselves in other programs to hide their presence. Once in a system, they may alter registry settings, so that they start automatically whenever the system is started.

More and more, we see that modern malware is not designed to damage systems, but rather to provide a way for an attacker to gather information about a target, or provide the opportunity for the attacker to gain access to the target at any time in the future.

Spreading malware

The original method of distributing malware was via floppy disk (sometimes called the "sneaker-net"). This idea has not disappeared; a lot of malware still spreads via USB sticks or other portable storage media. In the past decades, a lot of malware was spread via e-mail attachments (including that for the attack on RSA). An unsuspecting user that opens an e-mail attachment containing a virus is immediately infected by that virus. Another popular method of distributing malware is by infecting a user that visits a malicious website. Several forms of malware will use more than one method of distribution in order to be more successful.

The Stuxnet worm represented a major development in the evolution of malware, since it targeted programmable logic controllers (PLCs) – a high profile target not previously targeted. Over the next few years, we may see a lot of malware targeting new systems, such as smartphones, SCADA networks, Voice over IP (VOIP), and mobile applications.

Viruses

Early viruses: The first virus, "Brain," was developed over 25 years ago. Many of the early viruses were boot-sector infectors and would spread by replacing the boot sector of a floppy disk with infected code. Later viruses were more potent and learned to spread via networks and e-mail. A virus traditionally required the user to perform some action to trigger it – such as opening an attachment, or installing a portable media device.

Macro viruses: A macro virus infects via the macro capability of office software – often attaching itself to a document or spreadsheet.

Stealth viruses: A stealth virus attempts to hide its identity by changing subject lines, or altering or encrypting its code.

Polymorphic viruses: A polymorphic virus mutates itself, so that it changes slightly with each infection. By doing this, it attempts to hide from anti-virus engines that are looking for a specific virus signature.

Compression viruses: A compression virus executes when its code is decompressed.

Multipartite viruses: A multipartite virus is one that may circulate in several different ways and may spread more than one type of infection. Code Red and Nimda were examples of viruses that worked in a pair to leverage the security hole created when a system was infected by their pair virus.

Worms

A virus usually required the user's action to trigger the virus and launch the payload, but a worm usually spread on its own, normally by exploiting a vulnerability in software. SQL Slammer was an example of a worm that exploited a vulnerability in unpatched systems. It spread across the world, infecting over 70,000 machines in the first ten minutes of its life.

Logic bombs

A logic bomb is a type of malware that will trigger at a specific event or a time. A logic bomb can lie dormant on an infected machine for years, waiting for a certain condition to be met before it triggers. Some examples of logic bombs would trigger on a date or when a certain file was created.

Spyware and adware

Spyware is used for surveillance and captures activity on a system. Spyware can record valuable information for an attacker, including passwords, sensitive data and user behaviors. Companies also use surveillance software to record the activity of employees.

Trojan horses

A Trojan horse is a malicious program that is hidden within another program or utility. The Trojan is malicious, but the program it is hidden in appears to be useful or attractive to the user. Trojans are often hidden in documents, music or video files, photographs or bitmaps. The user may be tricked into accepting a Trojan by opening or downloading the seemingly useful program it is hidden in.

Zombies and botnets

A common problem today is the presence of massive, robotically controlled networks (or botnets) that consist of thousands (or, in some cases, over one million) compromised machines. A botnet is created by infecting vulnerable machines with a *zombie* program, which listens for commands issued by the owner of the botnet from a central command and control centre. The bot-herder or controller of the botnet can use the infected machines to perform various functions, such as the distribution of spam and distributed denial-of-service (DDoS) attacks.

In most cases, the owners of the infected machines that are part of a botnet are not even aware that their machine is a part of an illegal network. A person becomes a part of a botnet when they do not have adequate protection for their machine and it allows an attacker to infect their machine with the zombie agent. It is only through the deployment of security tools and patches that a potential victim can avoid being infected.

Denial of service (DoS) / distributed denial-of-service (DDoS) attacks

A denial of service prevents a user from using their systems or equipment. Many types of malware cause a denial of service – from the old "ping of death" attack that would cause equipment to fail by sending a mal-formed ping packet, to the SYN flooding attacks used to overwhelm networks and web servers.

One of the most challenging attacks to prevent has been the distributed denial-of-service attack. In a DDoS attack, the attack is amplified by using many machines (often in a botnet) to attack a target simultaneously. Such attacks are difficult to prevent or to stop, as was seen in the DDoS attack against the IP addresses for the country of Estonia in 2007[14]. Given the size of botnets available today, it would be very simple to launch an attack against a country or company that would render it totally isolated from web-based communications.

The DDoS attack is one of the new attack vectors being developed. Further information about this can be found in an excellent book by Richard A. Clarke: *Cyber War: The Next Threat to National Security and What to Do About It,* HarperCollins (2010)[15].

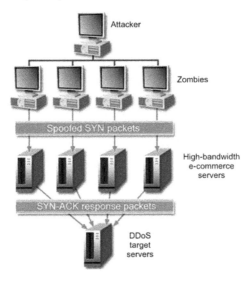

Figure 18: DDoS attacks

---

[14] http://arstechnica.com/security/news/2007/05/massive-ddos-attacks-target-estonia-russia-accused.ars.
[15] www.amazon.com/Cyber-War-Threat-National-Security/dp/0061962236/ref=pd_sim_b_5.

As seen in the above diagram, the attack is "amplified" by having many compromised computers participate in the attack. This makes the attack much more powerful, and also helps hide the true source of the attack.

Liability

If an organization's machines are used in the perpetrating of illegal activity that may cause damage to another party, there is a risk that the source organization may be held liable for damages caused. Therefore, all organizations must watch for the traffic outgoing from their firewalls to ensure that malicious traffic is not originating from within their internal network. This is where tools, such as Netcat,® which monitors the types of traffic that are passing through the network perimeter of the organization, can be helpful. The organization must also review its registry settings manually to detect any suspicious executables that have been installed into the registry.

Countermeasures

The most effective countermeasure for malicious code is user training. There are no tools or technology that can avoid infection if the users commit an improper act, such as opening a malicious e-mail attachment. The next step is to have a current anti-virus program that is used to monitor network traffic and scan hosts on a regular basis with the latest anti-virus signatures.

Reporting on the vulnerability assessment

The results of the VA and the ranking of the various vulnerabilities can be presented to the organization as a valuable review of their current security posture, or can be used in the next step of the pen test: the actual attempt to exploit the identified vulnerabilities. The report should also include a note of any unpatched systems or other administrative weaknesses.

Key learning points

A vulnerability assessment is one of the most important steps in evaluating the security profile and posture of the organization. Every organization should perform regular reviews and vulnerability assessments of their security and control framework to ensure that they are not vulnerable to new or emerging threats, and that the controls they have in place are working effectively.

The tester should use tools, but combine those tools with their own experience and expertise to ensure that the results of the assessments are accurate and meaningful.

Questions

1. A vulnerability assessment attempts to:
   a) Exploit any vulnerabilities in the network or systems found by the tester
   b) Focus on key areas of risk and known vulnerabilities in order to be more efficient
   c) Discover any weaknesses or flaws in the system being reviewed

d) Leverage the use of powerful tools in order to minimize human involvement.

Answer: C

2. From a security perspective, patch management is important to:
   a) Ensure system availability
   b) Protect the systems from new or emerging threats
   c) Defend the network equipment from application-based vulnerabilities
   d) Update all systems to improve performance and functionality.

Answer: B

3. The next step, following the use of a vulnerability assessment tool, is to:
   a) Report on the findings of the tool
   b) Analyze the results to determine the seriousness of the findings
   c) Immediately patch all serious identified vulnerabilities
   d) Perform a targeted penetration test.

Answer: B

4. Compliance with PCI DSS requires merchants that handle large numbers of transactions to conduct vulnerability assessments:
   a) Annually
   b) Quarterly
   c) Monthly

d) Weekly.

Answer: B

5. Common tools used in conducting a vulnerability assessment include:
   a) Nessus
   b) SANTA
   c) Eeye
   d) imap.

Answer: A

CHAPTER 6: HACKING WINDOWS® AND UNIX

Having fun

Ethical hacking is exploring, learning and discovery. It is the art of questioning, experimenting and persistence. An ethical hacker loves to learn; they are not interested in doing damage or harming another organization or individual, but rather looking for what new things may be found around the corner, under the rock, or beside the pathway. The opposite are criminals or crackers, people that are seeking their own profit, satisfying their ego or exacting revenge. It is important to remember that we should never do anything just to do damage or harm another person or organization. It is good to learn and experiment, but it must be with the mind to improve systems, networks, performance, functionality and usability. Many of the tools we use are free and were created as open source products by people from all over the world. These people work together to push each other to develop better and better products, and yet never withhold the benefits of their discoveries from others or try to make a profit from their work. Over the next few pages, we will examine many of the tools and features discovered by hackers, but we must remember to always use these with care and only within authorized boundaries. Since we are working to prevent an attacker from gaining entry to our systems, we must be aware of the methods and objectives of an attacker that is trying to compromise our systems, networks and applications.

Common hacking initiatives

Keystroke loggers

Keystroke loggers do exactly what their name says: they capture keystrokes. A keystroke logger will record everything a person types – including user IDs, passwords, banking data and e-mails – and provide it to the person that installed the keystroke logger.

Keystroke loggers can be either hardware or software. Many hardware-based devices will plug into a serial or USB port, or be placed in the middle of the connection between the keyboard and the desktop. They will gather and store information until retrieved and read by the person that placed them. These can be very difficult to detect, since not many people are inclined to crawl under their desks to check their keyboard cables or what is plugged into the USB ports on the back of their machines on a daily basis. Software-based keystroke loggers can be even more difficult to detect without using some form of detection software that would notice the presence of the logging application. Since software-based units can be installed and monitored remotely, they are a favorite of many criminal groups attempting to commit identity theft or fraud. As seen in the earlier discussion on spyware, some companies will use keystroke loggers to monitor user behaviors.

Password cracking

The next typical target for a malicious attacker is user accounts with passwords. Perhaps the attacker has already managed to gather the user accounts during the earlier footprinting and enumeration phase, and now all the attacker needs to do is determine the passwords used for those user IDs. In some cases, the attacker may also have downloaded a copy of the password file with the hashed password values for each user password. In the end, the challenge for the attacker is to gain access – and using a legitimate user account is often the easiest way to gain that access.

When a user logs into a Windows® system, the user password is hashed and stored as a hash value in a password file (a SAM or AD file). A hash is a value that is computed from the password that was entered by the user using a hashing algorithm (such as MD4). The hashing function is a one-way function – the hash is generated from the password, but the hash itself cannot be reverse-engineered back to learn what the original input password was. The challenge for the attacker is to learn what password value to enter that would produce the same hash value that is stored in the password file.

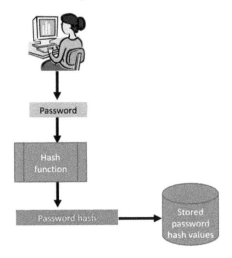

Figure 19: Password hashing

Dictionary and rainbow table attacks

The attacker may use several methods and several different tools to attack user accounts. Beyond just capturing passwords through keystroke loggers or intercepting them when sniffing (eavesdropping) on a network, the attacker may simply try all possible password values. This is called a brute-force attack, and it is the reason that most password entry systems will only allow a few possible entries before locking out the account. Another type of attack is to select a list of common words that people may have chosen as their password and try to access a user account using those as the password entries. This is called a dictionary attack. Some of the common dictionary attack tools will use common words from several languages and substitute letters for other symbols (A for @, e for 3, h for 4, 0 for O, etc.) When a user selects a simple password, password-cracking tools can break that password quite easily.

Another type of attack is based on pre-computed password hashes. These tables, called "rainbow tables" consist of entire lists of password hashes and the input values that would generate those hash values. Once the attacker has a copy of the password file, they can simply compare the stored hash values with the hash values in the rainbow table. A match on the hash would tell the attacker which input would generate that same hash. This type of attack is more difficult if the system uses a salt value (an extra input that is added to the password before hashing) together with the input password when generating the password hash.

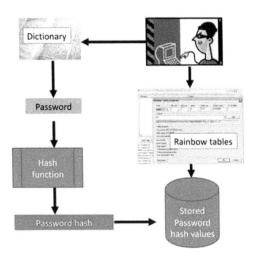

Figure 20: Rainbow tables

Defeating data theft

One of the most serious attacks an organization can suffer is the theft of sensitive data – such as credit card values, personally identifiable information (PII) or trade secrets. Theft of portable media is one of the most common ways an organization can lose sensitive data. The impact of a stolen laptop, for example, is equal to much more than just the cost of the laptop itself – it is the value of the data that was on the laptop that matters most. Loss of sensitive data may pose a large liability through financial penalties or damage to the reputation of the organization. One report by the security company Kensington documented that nearly half of all attacks against an organization originate from a laptop stolen from that organization.

A necessary security measure is to encrypt the data stored on the hard drive of the laptop or on any other portable storage media, including USB flashdrives.

Full disk encryption will automatically encrypt all the data stored on the hard drive. This makes it computationally infeasible for a person that gains access to a lost or stolen drive from being able to recover the data that is on the drive.

The deployment of hard drive encryption must ensure that the system will only boot up to a pre-boot security screen. If the system boots up to a normal screen, then it is possible for the attacker to steal the encryption key from RAM.

Protecting against unauthorized access

The most effective protection for a system is to ensure that only authorized personnel are able to gain access to the system and that, once on the system, the user is only granted the correct level of access needed for them to perform their job duties. This is the practice of the principles of "least privilege" and "need to know."

The principle of access control is based on the Identification, Authentication, Authorization, Accounting (IAAA) model.

Identification

Being able to identify a user or process that is requesting access to the system is integral to the protection of the system from unauthorized use. The challenge is in correctly identifying a user that is logging in, which is especially difficult when the user is logging in remotely over an untrusted network. The first principle must be to ensure that every user is uniquely identified – there must be no shared user IDs – and to ensure that a user ID is only provided to a user through a defined and well-managed process. Various studies have alleged that over half of the user IDs on corporate systems are set up incorrectly or are for personnel that no longer need them. Just like an open port on a firewall, every user ID that is left open is a potential point of attack.

Authentication

To authenticate is to validate or verify that the person presenting the user ID is who they say they are. The purpose of authentication is to prevent one person from using another person's user ID. There are three primary methods of authentication: asking what you know (knowledge), what you have (ownership), and what you are (biometrics). We also see node authentication where access is limited to a predefined MAC address, IP address or CPU serial number.

We are most familiar with knowledge-based authentication through the use of passwords, passphrases, or an answer to a "secret" question (often based on personal history or preferences).

Ownership-based authentication requires possession of a device – a token, smartcard or radio frequency identifier (RFID) chip. Most ownership-based approaches are either synchronous or asynchronous. Synchronous-based systems are based on time or events. The user requesting access must be able to respond to the authentication server with a value generated by their token. The value on the token will change every minute or two, or else will generate a new value every time the token is queried. The authentication server knows the value that should be displayed on the token at any point in time. Other ownership-based systems may require a USB token or serial port device to be plugged into the system, or an access card to be inserted into a reader, before granting access to a user.

Authenticating via characteristics is based on biometrics. Biometric devices are based on the characteristics of a person – their fingerprint, or retina or iris scan – or on behaviors, such as signature or voiceprints, or keystroke dynamics. The management and costs associated with biometric devices, as well as the reluctance of some users to be subject to biometric authentication, means that care must be taken when choosing to deploy a biometric-based system.

Multi-factor authentication

No single type of authentication is good enough to provide adequate security today. As seen earlier, it can be simple to break passwords, and users are often negligent in protecting passwords or tokens. The solution to this is to use more than one authentication type when granting access. The use of a password (or pin) and a token, or a token and a biometric makes it much more difficult for the attacker to break in. It is important to note that using two of the same type of mechanism (i.e. a token and a smartcard) is considered only single-factor authentication by the payment card industry (PCI).

Authorization

Authorization refers to the rights or permissions a user has on the system once they have been authenticated as a rightful user. Authorization should be set to only allow the minimum level of permission required by the user. A user that only needs read access, should not be granted write access, for example; and a user that is not required to delete files should not be granted that level of privilege.

Accounting

Accounting – sometimes called auditing – is the tracking and logging of the activity on the system. Every activity should be tracked to the user ID of the process that initiated the activity. This will allow an administrator to trace any activity on the system and associate that activity with the correct user. It is important that an attacker or user cannot alter or delete the logs to hide their mistakes or malicious activity.

Access controls

The most central or core concept of security is that security is centered on the principles of access control. Protecting a system, data or an organization is simply controlling who can do what, when and where they can do it, and what they can access. Access controls are made up of technical, physical and administrative (or managerial) controls.

As seen above, access starts with knowing who or what is trying to get onto the system. We can say that the entity that is trying to get access is the "subject." The subject is active and initiates an access request.

The entity or resource that the subject is attempting to access can be called the "object." An object provides a service and is passive in that it waits for a request to come from a subject before responding.

The secret is to put in place the rules that will govern how a subject can access an object. Often, the level of access provided will depend on the location of the subject, the group the subject belongs to, the roles or responsibilities of the subject, and the time of day (temporal controls).

Actions of the attacker

Once the attacker has gained access, they will often do several actions to hide their tracks and provide an easy method to break in in the future.

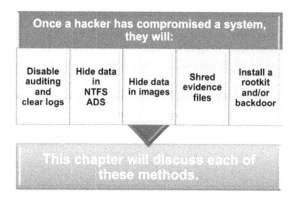

Figure 21: Hiding their tracks

The attacker does not want to be noticed – that would result in the system being repaired, denying them future access. The attacker, therefore, will attempt to hide their tracks and provide themselves an easy way in for the future through a rootkit *(see page 101)* or backdoor.

Sweeping away the footprints / clearing the logs

The attacker will often take steps to ensure that there is no evidence of their presence left behind. The logs and other records of their presence may be seen by an administrator and alert the organization to the attack. The attacker may attempt to hide their activity by temporarily disabling the logging features on the system, or erasing any evidence that was written to the logs.

To prevent this, the administrator may set the log files to be written to a write-once / read-many device, so that it is not possible for logs entries to be erased.

An attacker will also want to ensure that no evidence of the attack that would be discoverable in a forensics investigation is left on their host machine either To do this, they will shred any files or data that has been saved on their machine, including data or files stored in cache or temporary files.

In launching the attack, an attacker can hide their location through the use of products, such as Tor,® which will route their communications traffic through numerous hosts and make it very difficult for anyone to trace back the true source of the communications. Attackers will also use encrypted sessions to communicate with a target machine, since the encryption will render any firewalls, intrusion detection systems (IDSs) and intrusion prevention systems (IPSs) ineffective.

Hiding data

Attackers also take advantage of many of the tools and features built into operating systems for the benefit of administrators and maintenance. The use of these tools and features for malicious purposes is what we can call a "misuse case." A misuse case is where a tool or function that was intended for a beneficial purpose is misused for a negative reason. For example, the ping protocol is valuable to the administrator, but has been misused by attackers to conduct network mapping or to launch a denial-of-service attack by misconfiguring the ping protocol to create the "ping of death" attack.

Other features that are frequently misused by attackers are the alternate data fields associated with other documents – such as the alternate data stream in NTFS® files – in which attackers are able to hide information. It is possible to hide executable programs and other malicious data in a file (such as a document file or text file), so that it is not detectable using normal Windows® tools, such as Internet Explorer.® Malicious individuals will often use this technique to send, from one location to another, data that would only look like a normal file to a person reviewing it. This method is closely related to another activity called "steganography" – a common action used to hide information, rootkits or other malicious activity in music, jpeg or other bitmap files. The user of the steganography tool (of which there are several available as freeware on the Internet) "steals" the least significant bit (LSB) of the bytes in the file and uses those bits to carry their message. It is quite difficult to detect any files that have been used for steganographic communication.

Rootkits

A rootkit provides high-level access to a system (at root level) and would enable the controller of the rootkit to perform nearly any desired function on the target system. An attacker will often attempt to plant a rootkit onto a target system, since that will allow them unregulated access to that system at any time in the future. Once into the compromised system, they virtually "own" the systems and can do whatever actions they desire and remain undetected. Most rootkits are difficult to detect and require a complete rebuild of the system to be eradicated. There are several versions of rootkits that will provide this backdoor into a system.

Focus on UNIX/Linux

No system is impermeable or completely resistant to an attack. Every system has flaws and vulnerabilities that can be exploited by a malicious individual, and UNIX is no exception. (Neither is MAC, but that is a discussion for another time).

The attacks against *NIX systems are similar to those against Windows® systems: password cracking, escalation of privileges and theft of data. Whether the risk is of passwords being cracked in a brute-force attack, or system vulnerabilities being compromised through services that are available on the system, the most effective countermeasures are training, enforcing strong password rules, hardening the system and making sure that all patches have been deployed.

Common flaws in UNIX systems include exploits of file shares, kernel-based programming flaws, and shared libraries. The attacker is able to target any one of these weaknesses as they plan an attack.

Advanced attacks

The key goal of an attacker is to gain control over a system. This is usually accomplished by getting admin- or root-level access to the system and then installing backdoors that will allow the attacker unrestricted access to the system in the future. Many attacks are not simply conducted by brute-force attacks or "hammering away" at the system until something breaks. Instead, the attacks are often the result of a chain of exploits – each exploit opening the door for another potential avenue of attack. We see that many of the successful attacks against major corporations are accomplished through a series of concerted attacks that continue probing until the attacker finally overcomes all the defenses and is granted access to the key assets of the organization. We see that many attacks are focused not on the theft of credit card or other sensitive, personally identifiable information, or just embarrassing the target, but rather concentrate on the theft of corporate data, espionage and compromising trade secrets.

As both the skill level of the attacker and the value of the intellectual property of organizations increase, it becomes more and more important to increase our diligence and watchfulness to ensure that our organizations do not become victims or casualties along the edge of the information highway.

Invalid input

In far too many cases, it is rather simple to attack an application or system, or run a successful pen test. Many applications, operating systems, utilities and communications protocols are easily compromised through improperly input data. We have all heard the expression "garbage in – garbage out" used to describe the data contamination and errors caused by invalid input data, but this is only a small part of the problem. Not putting adequate controls in place to detect and prevent invalid input from users can lead to business interruption, errors and inconvenience. Yet, the danger that such a lack of control presents to business operations is much less significant than the advantage it presents to the attacker. By manipulating data entry, the attacker may be able to gain high-level access to the system or data, posing a risk far beyond that of simple data contamination or business inconvenience.

Database basics

A database acts as a large filing cabinet, but one with many added benefits. If a user wants to retrieve information from a filing cabinet, they must have physical access to it – which often means that several people located in different geographic locations will have their own files. This leads to duplications of information, but also, more seriously, inconsistencies in the data. One data source may be updated, but others will still be left with older versions.

Using a database to store all the data related to a project, customer, or other entity can provide global access and ensure that everyone is working from the same data source.

The mechanism that maintains and handles the database is the database management system (DBMS). The DBMS is like a filing clerk that maintains all the data on behalf of the other users. The DBMS is excellent at keeping the data organized and searching and retrieving data when required.

ISBN	Book name	Author ID	Price ($)	Genre	Type
0001-00	Computer Security	023	39.99	Technology	Hardcover
002-00	Economics	038	49.99	Business	Hardcover
003-00	Visit Italy	082	19.99	Travel	Softcover

Figure 22: Database example

The structure of the database is known as the *schema*. It describes how the data is defined and organized in terms of field sizes, allowable data values, etc.

In a relational database model, the data is stored in relations or tables. The data is grouped using a process called *normalization*. This ensures that a table only contains data that is properly related.

In most cases, a user cannot access the database directly, so they must use an application instead. This limits what the user can do, but, if it is not properly secured, the application can still be a vector for an attacker to gain access to the database.

The pen tester should know the basics of databases in order to test the security of the database architecture and ensure that no one can make improper changes to the data.

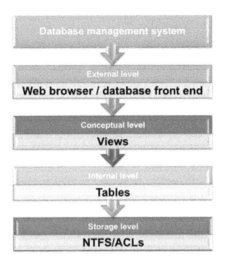

Figure 23: Database architecture

One of the challenges with web-based applications that interface with databases is that much of the processing is performed on the browser of the web client. Any data that is provided by a client can be modified by the client, so adequate controls have to be in place to prevent improper data entry or alteration.

The data in the database is arranged in rows or records and each record may contain many fields of data. Each row of a database may contain a large amount of data (for a customer, for example) and not every user needs to be able to see all of the data in the whole database. For this reason, the application will usually refer to the database using a view. The view is really a filter that restricts the information provided to the user, so that the user cannot even see the data fields where they do not have a "need to know."

Injection and manipulation

Structured Query Language (SQL) is a common language used to access information from a database. Many attackers target databases using SQL commands in order to provide themselves with access to unauthorized information. A recent audit performed for a major airport found that the airport's core systems were subject to more than 1000 SQL injection flaws (despite the assurances from the initial application developers that the applications were not vulnerable to SQL injection). The use of SQL injection to expose database contents and compromise a system has been a tool in the attackers' arsenal for over a decade, and yet there are still many applications in use – and even being built today – that are susceptible to SQL injection-based attacks. A pen tester should always test applications for this vulnerability. Many applications will accept user input – log-in information, for example – and insert that input into a pre-existing SQL statement in the code. The SQL statement is then executed and performs the function intended by the application developer (in this case, allowing the user to log in if they have input the correct log-in information). By inserting invalid data into the user input field, the attacker or pen tester can test whether the application was written to validate the user input prior to executing the SQL statement. If the input is not validated, and the SQL statement is executed, then whatever data the attacker put in that field will be executed. This may present the attacker with the entire contents of the database or access to other information or areas that were never intended by the application developer.

Figure 24: SQL injection

This is an example of code that may be running on the SQL server:

```
SELECT name, phone, address, bank details FROM tblLogins
WHERE
name = '              '  AND password = '              ';
```

The white spaces represent the user input fields on the database front end, although they are actually variables containing some value.

```
SELECT name, phone, address, bank_details FROM tblLogins
WHERE
name = ' & varname & ' AND password = ' & varpassword & ';
```

The data entered into the user input field will be used to build the complete SQL statement, but an attacker may not enter a username and password!

By entering (injecting) a positive statement like ' OR 1=1;--, anyone can bypass the login authorization!

```
Select name, phone, address, bank details FROM tblLogins
WHERE
name = ' ' OR 1=1;-- 'AND password ='       ';
```

What does it all mean?

'	Closes the user input variable
OR	Continues the SQL statement
1=1	A true statement
;	Finishes the statement
–	Indicates that everything after the dashes is a comment and the rest of the line is not processed.

The server wants a balance between the value name and the user input.

We give it 1=1, so that is 'sees' a balance and logs us on as the first account in the table.

By inserting unauthorized data into the name and password fields, the attacker is able to access the database.

Other injection attacks are made possible by inserting stored procedure or shutdown commands into the SQL statement.

Protecting databases

Protecting a database starts with the same types of protection normally used for other systems and equipment: changing default settings, enforcing strong password rules and disabling unneeded services. This protection should be augmented by setting up a tiered architecture – so that users have to access the data through an application and cannot access a database directly – validating all input to the database, and using parameterized queries that restrict the values that a user can enter into a SQL statement.

A good resource to help protect databases and web applications is the Open Web Application Security Project or OWASP (*www.owasp.org*).

Format string

The application developer is naturally focused on delivering the required business functionality, and is often unaware of the risks associated with misuse cases (where an attacker could misuse that functionality for their own purposes). The aim of the pen tester is to find any security flaws in the target system that could be exploited by an attacker. To do this, the pen tester will test for misuse cases and not just test the proper function of the system. The pen tester does this by testing applications and any user input fields with strange data – data that would not normally have been input by a proper user – to see if the application has been written to detect and reject such invalid input correctly.

Some programming languages are more vulnerable to invalid input than others, especially those that will do formatting of data automatically. The C programming language is a good example of this. Several functions, such as "printf", will execute without validating input and may, therefore, be manipulated by an attacker to overwrite other memory areas or corrupt system operations.

Buffer overflows

Buffer overflow attacks have been one of the most common problems found in systems programming over the years. A buffer overflow condition is caused when the data being written into memory exceeds the space allotted to it. This could happen if, for example, an input field that has been set to eight characters in length is filled in with data exceeding eight characters in length by an attacker. If the program does not check the size and content of the data being provided, it may write the input data into memory – putting the first eight characters into the properly allocated memory space, but then continuing to write into the next memory areas and overwriting whatever content was originally there. This becomes especially dangerous when the content being supplied by the attacker overwrites memory pointers or contains executable code.

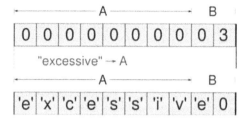

Figure 25: Buffer overflows

In this example, we can see that the memory allocated to the field "A" was set to eight characters, but the input provided to the system (the word "excessive") is nine characters in length. This caused field "B" to be changed from its correct value of "03" to a new value of "e0." The program is most likely to fail or process incorrectly, since it may not know how to process an alphabetic value in a numeric field.

Verifying that an application or system will not accept invalid inputs is one of the most important parts of a pen test. The tester must try all types of valid and invalid input to ensure that an attacker cannot cause the system to fail or be compromised through manipulation of input data. The test should try various input styles as well. For example, data could be input in Unicode (instead of in ASCII characters), the same values could be input in different ways (canonicalization), or alternate character sets of languages could be used.

Fuzzing

When testing an application, the pen tester will frequently use techniques, such as "fuzzing," to test the ranges accepted and the application's ability to handle unexpected input values. Fuzzing is the use of inexact data, incomplete data, and data that is outside of expected ranges to test whether an application can resist and handle invalid input.

Memory management

As seen in the discussion on buffer overflows, exploiting memory management is one of the most popular angles of attack that can be used against many operating systems. Memory is allocated in two forms: heap and stack. As data is moved into memory, it requires pointers and links to other memory areas. If an attacker can manipulate their input data to overwrite those pointers or links, they may cause their input data to execute as if it was a part of the original program commands located in those memory spaces.

Error handling

A common approach for attackers is to intentionally cause an error or exception to a process. It is common to find that the error handling process used by the developer will provide information that may enable an attacker to adjust or tune their attack to be more effective. This error handling approach is usually chosen by the application developer in order to allow them to identify the cause of an error and facilitate the correction of the problem. However, the attacker benefits from the information provided, as well. For this reason, any error handling code should be masked by using error codes or by just providing generic information.

Source code review

A pen test may include a review of the source code for the applications used by the organization. This type of review requires both a specialized skill set that many pen testers may not have and access to the source code itself – not always possible with vendor-supplied programs or to external pen testing teams.

A source code review looks at the actual program code itself to identify flaws in the program logic or bugs in the code itself.

Ideally, the first review of the source code will have been conducted during the design and development phases of the Systems (or Software) Development Life Cycle (SDLC®). As applications mature, changes are made to applications or system configurations, the threat environment evolves, and the operational world and user environment adjusts, it is important to review the programs to ensure that they remain secure, that the controls are operating correctly, and that the system continues to be resistant to attack.

A source code review examines the code for improper error handling, buffer overflow conditions, logic flaws and efficiency. The reviewer should approach the source code review from both a use-case (testing what the program was intended to do) and a misuse-case perspective (assessing the attack surface area, the possible points of attack or misuse, etc.). The review should especially focus on program areas that handle sensitive data and ensure that security controls – such as encryption, authentication and logging – are working correctly.

All of the following should be considered in data validation:

- Weak validation is the reason most attacks are successful. Make sure the application is validating the data for:
  - Type
  - Format
  - Length
  - Range
  - Valid business values.
- Data should be validated before constructing SQL statements.
- It should be validated that output does not contain scripting characters.

Log files

Logs are detective controls and, as such, cannot prevent an attack. But they can do two things:

1. Deter an attack if the attacker knows that their activity will be noticed
2. Aid in the investigation of a possible attack or mistake by a user.

It is not uncommon to find that log files are one of the most overlooked and ineffective security controls available to an organization. Frequently, organizations store copious amounts of data in log files and then never review it. Another mistake is to store the wrong data – most of which is of little use when an attack happens.

In a world of regulation and privacy legislation, it is the responsibility of the organization to prove that their controls over data confidentiality and integrity are adequate and meeting the requirements of the regulations[16]. The logs should provide a historical record of all activity on the system – especially when it concerns access or changes to sensitive data.

The following is a list of questions and issues to consider when conducting a log file review:

- Are all login attempts being logged? Both successful and unsuccessful attempts should be logged.
- Is logging centralized? Using a centralized approach encourages consistency and code re-use.
- What is being logged?
  - Is sensitive information being logged and, if so, what protection measures are in place to prevent the log files from disclosure?
- Does the log file allow scripting tags to be written? Cross-site scripting should be avoided.
- Are the logs protected from being erased or overwritten?
- Are the log files large enough to prevent application failure in case they are subject to flooding?

Authentication

Protecting systems from errors, abuse, and compromise starts with ensuring that only the correct people are on the system, and that they can only perform authorized actions once they have been granted access. As seen earlier, this involves the following steps: entity identification (determining who or what is requesting access); authentication (validating or verifying that the entity is who

---

[16] *www.bcauditor.com/pubs/2010/report7/paris-system-community-care-services-access-and-security*.

they say they are); authorization (controlling what rights, privileges and permissions a user has once they are on the system); and accounting (logging and recording all activity on the system and associating that activity with the entity that performed it).

As was also seen earlier, there are three primary methods of authenticating an entity requesting access: by confirming something they know, something they have, or something they are. Unfortunately, all three of these methods are subject to compromise – they can be defeated or bypassed by an attacker that can steal a password or token, or copy a biometric value. Therefore, it is necessary to use a combination of authentication techniques in order to validate the identity of the entity. This is called multi-factor authentication. The pen tester should ensure that this is in place on the target system. Any system that is only using single-factor authentication is susceptible to unauthorized access.

Account lockout

If an entity requests access (attempts to log in) to a system, they must be able to provide the correct response to the authentication mechanism – a password, smartcard or biometric signature, for example. If they do not respond correctly, the system should deny entry. It will, however, usually provide the applicant with an error code and an opportunity to answer again. Users frequently mistype or forget passwords, or read a CAPTCHA value incorrectly; in other instances, the biometric device may fail to authenticate the applicant correctly (commonly known as a "type one" error, or a "false reject rate"). Once a person has tried, unsuccessfully, to log in multiple times, it may be evident that the entity requesting access is not the person they claim to be – that they are attempting to masquerade or spoof their identity and gain unauthorized access. After the entity has tried to log in multiple times, the system should lock out the account and prevent any further log-in attempts from that account until it can be verified that only the correct person is attempting to use it. The question, however, is: what is an acceptable human error rate, and how would it compare with that of a brute-force attack? Should the system lock the account after one invalid password entry, or let the person attempt three, four or five times? The level or threshold at which action is taken to lock the account is called the "clipping level." An error rate below the threshold is discarded or clipped off, but once the threshold has been crossed, action is taken.

Case study: Attack on a Chinese bank[17]

The entire text of this attack can be found at the link provided.

A classic attack on a bank's authentication system was seen several years ago, when an attacker was able to execute a script against the bank's online application that allowed the attacker to log in to other users' accounts and transfer the money out of their accounts. The attacker knew that the clipping level for the bank's online log-in would only permit a few log-in attempts to an account before locking out the account. However, the system did not detect or react to a user that would attempt to log in using a different

---

[17] *www.isaca.org/Journal/Past-Issues/2007/Volume-5/Pages/A-Hacker-Breaks-In-Lessons-Learned-From-a-True-Story1.aspx*.

account number each time. The attacker selected a common word that was likely to be used by several people as their log-in password, and then wrote a script to try that password against all the user accounts on the system. The attacker found that five people had used that password as their online banking password and transferred their money to other accounts he had set up. He then withdrew the money from ATMs and various branches of the bank.

Some of the reasons for this attack being successful were:

* Poor session management, which locked an account after five unsuccessful attacks, but allowed a person to attempt multiple access attempts, as long as different account numbers were used
* Client-side authentication only, which allowed the attacker to modify some of the security controls being passed from the client to the server
* Single-factor authentication, which did not require any further verification from the entity requesting access.

Configuration management

Configuration files should also be checked for sensitive information, such as default user or password settings, and session management and other hardcoded data.

There are several products available to the tester to facilitate a source code review, but these tools are not a substitute for manual verification. A tool is excellent for finding simple coding flaws – unexecuted code, poor validation, etc, but is not effective at finding complex logic flaws or some types of injection attacks. Therefore, it is always preferable to deploy a combination of tools and conduct a manual review to audit source code and application logic.

Key learning points

This chapter dealt with many of the steps undertaken by an attacker to defeat the security control over a system – and, therefore, the topics that a pen tester must be aware of and test for when conducting a thorough pen test.

Key points covered include:

- Hacking versus pen testing: objectives and methods
- Keystroke loggers: software and hardware
- Password cracking: rainbow tables and dictionary attacks
- Protecting personally identifiable information (PII)
- Identification, Authentication, Authorization, Accounting (IAAA)
- Erasing and clearing logs
- Use and misuse case models
- Hiding data: alternate data streams and steganography
- Invalid inputs: canonicalization, buffer overflows, injection
- Memory management: heap versus stack
- Error and exception handling: verbose error code
- Source code review
- Logging activity
- Configuration review.

Questions

1. A pen test is designed to:
   a) Simulate the same type of activity as an attack
   b) Identify and repair any problems within a target system / application
   c) Ensure compliance with regulations or legislation
   d) Publicly expose any flaws or errors in the system configuration.

Answer: A

B is incorrect – a pen test does not fix the problems, it detects and reports on them. C is incorrect – publicly exposing any flaws or errors in the system configuration is the job of the compliance audit. D is incorrect – a pen test is confidential and only reports to the client organization.

2. A password cracking tool that uses predetermined hash values is a:
   a) Dictionary attack
   b) Canonicalization attack
   c) Hash injection attack
   d) Rainbow table.

Answer: D

Answer A uses common words; B and C are made up.

3. Which of the following is an example of personally identifiable information (PII)?
   a) Name
   b) Address
   c) Health data
   d) Education.

Answer: C

None of the other answers are considered to be PII.

4. Authorization should be based on:
   a) Multi-factor validation of identity
   b) Recording and tracking all activity on a system
   c) The principles of "need to know" and "least privilege"
   d) Ensuring that all users are uniquely registered on the system.

Answer: C

Answer A is authentication, answer B is accounting, and answer D is identification.

5. Error messages should always be:
   a) Detailed enough to permit troubleshooting
   b) Logged in a centrally managed database
   c) Protected from being overwritten or erased
   d) Generic, so as to not disclose data to an attacker.

Answer: D

Answer A is incorrect; a verbose error may provide an advantage to an attacker. Answer B is incorrect; errors need not be centrally recorded – activity logs may be centrally recorded. Answer C is incorrect; this relates to logs, not error messages.

6. Steganography is a method of:
   a) Hiding data in music or picture files
   b) Protecting sensitive data

c) Protecting the integrity of data through the creation of a computed hash value
d) Manipulating input data.

Answer: A

Answer B is incorrect – encryption is used to protect sensitive data. Answer C is incorrect – this is hashing. Answer D is incorrect – this is an injection attack.

7. A memory buffer overflow attack attempts to:
   a) Put more data in an input field than the field was designed to contain
   b) Prevent memory pointers from linking to the wrong programs
   c) Put SQL data into an input data field
   d) Flood a memory stack with SYN requests.

Answer: A

Answer B is incorrect – a buffer overflow may corrupt memory pointers. Answer C is incorrect – this is an SQL injection attack. Answer D is incorrect – a SYN flood attack floods a network, not a memory stack.

8. A source code review should be done following implementation because:
   a) This is the most effective time to review source code
   b) Changes to applications need to be reviewed to ensure the security configuration is still effective
   c) Tools can only work on code once it is implemented
   d) Errors in the business logic are easiest to detect once the system is operational.

Answer: B

The source code review should be done first – during design and development – but repeated once the system is implemented, in order to ensure that the security controls are still working correctly. The other answers are all correct when doing a source code review earlier in the SDLC process.

CHAPTER 7: LAUNCHING THE ATTACK

Steps to an exploit

The objective of most attackers is to try to take over a compromised system and assume an elevated level of access. One way to accomplish this is to obtain a command line shell that can be used to execute system commands and run malicious code on the compromised system. There are several types of command shells that are used for local or remote access.

Local shellcode: Local shellcode is used to provide the attacker with access to a local machine that would otherwise restrict the access level of the attacker.

Remote shellcode: Remote shellcode is used to facilitate an attack that the attacker is executing across a network or on a remote machine.

Restricting shellcode: Many firewalls and intrusion detection systems (IDSs) will detect shellcode. Therefore, the attacker must frequently attempt to hide the presence of the shellcode using obfuscation, encryption, or breaking the code into multiple segments.

Writing a shell is beyond many attackers; however, there are several tools that are available to make the job of the attacker easier, such as Metasploit® and SAINT.

These tools will assist the pen tester in locating vulnerabilities and then provide several methods that can be used to exploit the access granted by the system.

Attacking wireless networks

Case study: TJX

TJX believes the intruder may have initially gained access to customer information via the wireless local area networks at two of its US stores. Customer information was stolen from mid-2005 through December 2006, a TJX investigation found. Some stolen information involved transactions dating back to 2002.[18]

The theft at TJX (which targeted HomeSense and Winners, amongst other stores) led to the compromise of the personal information – credit card and driver's license details and banking data – of approximately 49 million people. This was an example of a chained exploit. The initial attack against the wireless networks in two stores in Miami, Florida, enabled a further attack against the Head Office itself. This attack demonstrates the importance of enforcing a security standard across the entire enterprise – a security hole in any one location may lead to a breach at other locations.

It has often been stated that having a wireless device in your office is the same as having an ethernet connection in your parking lot. This is not to say that the use of wireless should be discouraged or forbidden. We must secure the wireless access points we provide, just as we would a publicly available network connection.

---

[18] *www.priv.gc.ca/media/nr-c/2007/nr-c_070925_e.cfm.*

Evolution of wireless security

Wireless security has been attempted through several approaches. The first approach was to hide the service set identifier (SSID) of the wireless access point. The SSID is the name of the wireless access point and, by default, it is set to be broadcast out. That enables any other wireless device in the area to detect the presence of the device and allow it to attempt to log in. Far too often, the name of the SSID is either left as the default setting or set to a company name. This allows a person to identify either whom the access point belonged to, or "find" it by searching for the default names. The question came of whether or not the SSID should be set to broadcast at all; would it be better for it to rather sit silently and only react when a person that knew its name attempted to associate with it? Hiding the name is a form of "security by obscurity"; it is not very effective, but arguments can be made that it's better than doing nothing. Another approach taken by some companies was to intentionally broadcast the SSID, so that a legitimate employee trying to log in would know for sure that they were on the correct access point and not end up sending sensitive information over another rogue device.

Another level of security was the use of MAC filtering. The MAC address should be unique to each device; however, the MAC address is passed in the clear when a device attempts to associate with the access point. An attacker can easily determine the MAC address and spoof it to overcome that control. Using MAC filtering also places a heavy workload on the administrators when there are a lot of changes in personnel needing to be able to log in, since the MAC address for each device must be entered into the access table directly on demand.

The first wireless encryption that was available was provided through a standard known as Wired Equivalent Privacy (WEP). WEP used a good algorithm (RC4®), but in a poorly implemented manner. The initialization vector (IV) was too short and could be caused to repeat by flooding the access point with association requests. This made the "cracking" of the WEP key a fairly simple process.

When the vulnerability of WEP was found and disclosed, a quick fix was introduced. The new version was initially planned to be called WEP2, but was re-named Wi-Fi Protected Access® (WPA®) when it was thought that calling it WEP2 immediately after the weaknesses of WEP were disclosed would not inspire confidence!

WPA also used the RC4 algorithm and introduced the MIC integrity check and Temporary Key Integrity Protocol (TKIP). MIC provides some assurance that the packets are not being modified in some way as they are transmitted wirelessly, and TKIP improves the key generation process.

The next step in wireless encryption was the introduction of WPA2.® WPA2 uses the Advanced Encryption Standard (AES) algorithm in Counter mode, and uses CBC-MAC for integrity. This is commonly referred to as CCMP. WPA2 is a secure method of implementing wireless encryption and should be the standard for all organizations.

Pen testing wireless

Wireless devices pose a great risk to an organization if not implemented correctly – and they are often not. The usual problems, which are the same as those for almost all network devices, are: default configurations, weak passwords, encryption not being enabled at all, the continued use of WEP, and the installation of rogue wireless (unauthorized devices). Wireless devices, however, present an entirely new set of risks, as well. A wireless device can be attached to almost any point on a network, and an insecure or rogue device can be placed inside the firewall and provide an open, undefended door of opportunity onto the network for an attacker.

The first step in pen testing for wireless devices is to do the same as most attackers would do: walk around the physical location, detecting any wireless devices. This is often called "war-driving." Several tools – from Netstumbler® to Kismet® and the Aircrack-ng set of tools – can help detect wireless devices.

The next step is to check whether the wireless devices have default configurations, or if they are located in a DMZ or separate area that would restrict access from the wireless device to the internal network. A valuable resource that can help the administrator or pen tester to learn more about wireless security is the *www.wirelessdefence.org* website.

Denial of service

As wireless devices become more and more essential in the support of business operations, the impact of a denial-of-service attack increases. Unfortunately, wireless devices share the same radio frequency (RF) bands as many other devices – ranging from microwave ovens to cordless phones and toys. A wireless device is easily affected by other devices operating in the same RF band in close proximity. Common attacks can be the simple jamming of the RF signal.

Another common attack against wireless is the propagation of disassociate or de-auth packets. Sending either of these packets out with the MAC address of the target device will cause the device to temporarily disconnect itself from the network.

IEEE 802.1x and the Extensible Authentication Protocol (EAP)

One of the most challenging problems associated with wireless is in knowing who or what is trying to authenticate. Some of the common methods of authenticating a device are IEEE 802.1x, EAP-TLS, and EAP-TTLS. The older EAP is not recommended for deployment unless very long passwords are used. EAP-TLS and EAP-TTLS support public key certificates that provide server authentication and validate the identity of the supplicant (the wireless device requesting permission to associate) via a RADIUS authentication server.

Network sniffing

Network sniffing is the capturing of traffic traversing a network. Many administrators will sniff network traffic in order to detect traffic problems, bottlenecks and network traffic issues.

If an attacker is able to sniff the traffic, they may find sensitive data that is not encrypted, log-in and password information, and other data related to business operations and error handling.

There are a several good tools available for network sniffing and protocol analysis, as seen in the table below.

Program	Operating system	Source
Wireshark®	Windows® and UNIX	Free from *www.wireshark.org*
TCPDump	UNIX	Free from *www.tcpdump.org*
WinDump	Windows®	Free from *http://windump.polito.it*
OmniPeek®	Windows®	Purchase from *www.wildpackets.com*
Packetyzer®	Windows®	*www.network-chemistry-packetyzer.software.informer.com*
Cain & Abel	Windows®	Free from *www.oxid.it*

Figure 26: Examples of packet sniffers and protocol analyzers

Active versus passive sniffing

Passive sniffing is the capturing of data without injecting, deleting or modifying it. Eavesdropping is an example of passive sniffing. A person doing passive sniffing frequently wants to remain unnoticed and sit quietly on the line, capturing data without anyone knowing that they are there.

Active sniffing is done to make some change to a system or the data on the network. This may be achieved through efforts such as DNS poisoning, Address Resolution Protocol (ARP) cache poisoning, source routing or MAC spoofing.

A hacker has two choices for modifying the routing of packets:	
Control layer-two routing (ethernet routing) • Switching forwarding table flooding • ARP cache poisoning • MAC spoofing.	**Control layer-three routing (IP routing)** • DNS poisoning • Source routing • Advertising bogus routes • ICMP redirecting messages • Rogue DHCP servers.

Figure 27: Active sniffing

ARP poisoning allows the attacker to pose as a legitimate user on the network. The attacker will then be able to capture all the traffic that is being sent to the other user.

DNS spoofing

DNS spoofing has been a common attack to divert web traffic to illegitimate sites. The domain name server resolves the web address with an IP address. If an attacker can poison the DNS table, he will be able to have traffic intended for one location sent to another site of his choosing. This method has been used to divert the traffic for one business to another location, causing a denial of service and general embarrassment for the business. In the diagram which follows, you can see how diverting e-mail traffic would allow an attacker to intercept and monitor all traffic going from company B to company A.

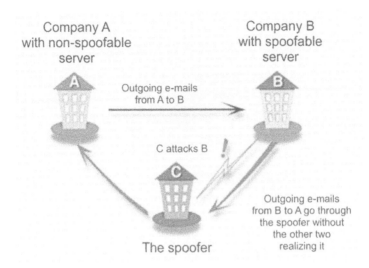

Figure 28: DNS spoofing

Session hijacking

Session hijacking allows an attacker to hijack or take over a legitimate session between two other entities. The attacker sniffs the session ID being used between two parties and then sends traffic to the receiver using the correct session ID. This can fool the receiving session into thinking that they are still connected with the legitimate user that set up the connection initially. The attacker now has access to the receiver as if they are a legitimate user.

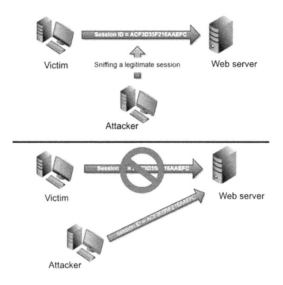

Figure 29: Session hijacking

Fake SSL sessions

SSL uses certificates to validate the web server being connected to. If an attacker can insert themselves into the middle of an SSL connection that is being set up (execute a man-in-the-middle attack (MITM) through DNS spoofing or ARP poisoning), then they may be able to intercept the certificate exchange and send a fake certificate to the originator – fooling the originator into thinking that they are securely connected to a legitimate site, when they are, in fact, connected to the attacker. This has also been done by creating a fake SSL certificate registered to a name similar to the legitimate name of the organization. One successful attack of this type was carried out by an attacker registering an SSL certificate to a ".org" version of the ".com" address that a company had their certificate registered to.

Intercepting VOIP

In the next few years, we can expect most organizations to move towards the use of Voice over IP (VOIP) for telephone calls. This method provides several benefits to an organization, including better integration between data and voice services and potential savings on long-distance calling. However, VOIP packets can be intercepted as they traverse a network. Tools, such as Cain & Abel, will collect and reassemble VOIP packets, so that the person monitoring the network can listen in on the conversation.

Countermeasures for sniffing

There are several countermeasures that can be used to prevent network sniffing. The first is to use encryption to make any traffic (including VOIP) that is captured worthless. Other precautions are to use an intrusion detection system (IDS) to log and alert staff to any abnormal traffic flows or suspicious traffic. The administrator should also be watching for ARP poisoning. Users should be educated to not accept any certificates that are not from a known source.

Firewalls

Firewalls are used between networks to protect one network from any suspicious activity originating from another, and to prevent any improper traffic from going out of a network.

Firewall types		
Generation one:	Packet filtering	
Generation two:	Proxy	
Generation three:	Stateful	
Generation four:	Dynamic packet filtering	
Generation five:	Kernal proxies	

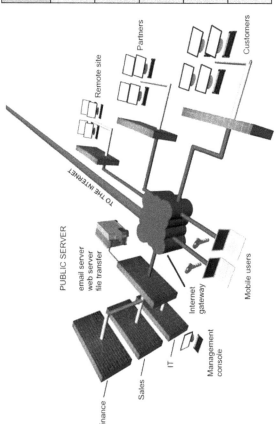

Figure 30: Firewalls

There are several types of firewalls, as seen in the table preceding. A firewall, however, is only as effective as the rules and administration used to set it up.

Network and firewall architecture

Networks should be protected in a layered defense model, with layers of control and defenses to protect the assets of the organization.

The core principle is that no traffic should be allowed from an untrusted network – such as the Internet – directly into the internal network. A demilitarized zone (DMZ) is an isolated network area that can be used by the organization to provide some restricted or limited services to clients gaining access from the Internet. An extranet is also an isolated network area, but it is usually used for providing services to business partners, and requires additional authentication or log-in (compared with that needed for a DMZ).

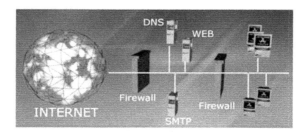

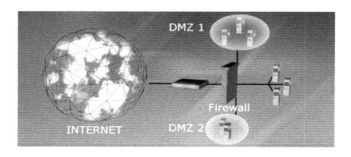

Figure 31: Firewall architecture

Circumventing firewalls

There are several methods used to circumvent firewalls, including fragmentation (breaking the elements of the attack into small pieces that may not be noticed by the firewall) and causing subsequent fragments to overlap previous fragments on reassembly. Often, the firewall is "blinded" by using encryption, so that the firewall cannot see what the content of the packet is.

Intrusion detection and prevention systems (IDS/IPS)

Intrusion detection systems are valuable network and host defense tools. An IDS will attempt to notice any suspicious activity (floods, protocol anomalies, or known malicious signatures) and log the event. The IDS may also alert an administrator or signal other devices to a potential problem. The IPS is more proactive and will attempt to stop any unauthorized activity. IDSs and IPSs should be used in combination with firewalls and other defensive tools in a layered defensive model. They may be network-based and used to monitor the activity on a network, or they may be host-based and watch for unauthorized activity on a host.

Key learning points

- Shellcode is often used by attackers to gain elevated system access. There are several types of shellcode, including local and remote shellcode.
- Shellcode can be detected by a firewall or IDS.
- Metasploit and SAINT are two tools used by attackers to gain privileged system-access.
- Wireless security has been provided by disabling SSID broadcasting, MAC filtering, IEEE 802.1x port controls, EAP, encryption and integrity checks.
- WEP and WPA use RC4 for encryption; WPA2 uses Advanced Encryption Standard – Counter with Cipher Block Chaining Message Authentication Code Protocol (AES-CCMP).
- War-driving is enabled by tools like Kismet, Netstumbler and the Aircrack-ng set of tools.
- Denial of service on a wireless can be accomplished by jamming the signal or flooding the network.

Questions

1. What form of integrity checking was used in WPA?
   a) RC4
   b) AES
   c) Michael (MIC)
   d) CCMP.

Answer: C

2. An effective measure to protect a wireless from unauthorized access from outside the building is to deploy:
   a) Radio frequency (RF) management
   b) SSID broadcasting
   c) Michael (MIC)
   d) RC4.

Answer: A

3. A wireless access point located near a microwave oven may be subject to:
   a) MAC filtering
   b) Open system authentication
   c) ARP poisoning
   d) Denial-of-service jamming.

Answer: D

4. Wireless access points operate in the radio frequency ranges of:
   a) 900 – 1900 Mhz
   b) 2.4 – 5 Ghz

c) 900 Mhz – 2.4 Ghz
d) 2.4 Ghz – 1900Ghz.

Answer: B

5. In order to protect internal networks, it is best to:
   a) Place all wireless access points directly on internal networks
   b) Have strict policies forbidding the use of wireless access points
   c) Disable the wireless modems in all laptops
   d) Install securely configured wireless access points in a demilitarized zone (DMZ).

Answer: D

CHAPTER 8: ATTACKING WEB APPLICATIONS

The Web provides business opportunities that would have been unimaginable only a decade or so ago. Every organization can reach customers globally and provide service, support and communications for clients, employees and business partners – no matter where in the world they are and what time zone they are in. However, the Web is also open for attack 24 hours a day, seven days a week. Attackers can pose a threat to an organization from any country, without ever stepping a foot in the country the organization operates in.

For the most part, hackers are lazy and will gravitate towards making the easiest types of attack. For that reason, we see instances where organizations have a common vulnerability for several years but remained unhurt. The attackers do not find the vulnerability and the organization may even believe that they are secure, since no one is successfully attacking them. The reality, however, is just that the hackers are missing the vulnerability. When the first security breach is finally found, then – like wolves circling wounded prey – the hackers converge on the newly discovered victim and, often, will expose dozens of security vulnerabilities within a few weeks.

The route to an attack is often challenging for the attacker. They must overcome layers of defense and multiple obstacles that are intended to make an attack difficult and capture any information about an ongoing attack. As seen in the diagram below, the attacker must often know how to circumvent multiple technologies before they reach their ultimate goal. Firewalls, network partitions, anti-virus software, IPS and access controls will all attempt to deter or prevent the attack from succeeding.

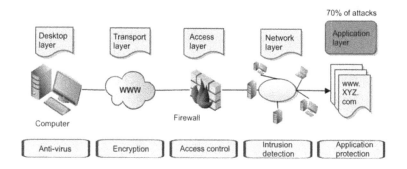

Figure 32: Overcoming layered defense

When an organization – such as a bank, for example – was only operating in a physical (bricks and mortar) world, the one way to steal money from it was through physical access. A thief had to either be physically present at the location to make an unauthorized withdrawal, or they had to have access to the transportation network that was carrying money to or from the bank. It would have been extremely difficult for a thief in one country to have robbed money from a bank in another country – unless they travelled to the country where the victim bank was. Then came the Web. Banks (as just one example) realized the opportunities that online services could provide. Now, people can access their accounts anytime and from anywhere. The only problem here is that everyone else has the opportunity to access the bank's online system as well – so any vulnerabilities in the configuration of the bank's networks or applications, or in the security of the client's browsers, become a road of opportunity for an attacker.

Now, a thief in one country is able to probe, evaluate and exploit any vulnerabilities in a banking system anywhere in the world. Furthermore, it is questionable if the current legal frameworks and law enforcement personnel are adequate to investigate and prosecute such attacks. After all, if an attacker in country "A" routes through several networks in countries "B" and "C" to attack a bank in country "D," where can it be said the crime was committed? At the location of the victim, or the attacker? And will law enforcement be able to gather the information required from the intermediary countries to investigate and trace the crime? These problems are some of the reasons that web applications have become one of the most frequent places of attack. In fact, it is estimated that up to 70% of all attacks today are focused on web applications. An application is open 24 hours a day, seven days a week, and the protection in front of it is often inadequate: the firewall may be open on ports 80 and 443 to allow traffic to reach the web server; the attack may be encrypted, so that it cannot be read by the IPS and firewall; or the client's system my be compromised. Moreover, an application is the conduit to all the data and business information located in the background on databases, files and servers.

The steps in attacking a web application

An attack against a web application starts in much the same way as any other attack on an organization: scanning and reconnaissance; information gathering; testing; planning the attack; and launching the attack. Starting with scanning for open ports and services, the attacker will gather as much information as possible about the web service – the operating system, the structure of the uniform resource locator (also known as the universal resource locator, or URL), the file structures, and the business functions allowed – and then test for obvious vulnerabilities. Once a potential vulnerability has been found, the attacker will plan and execute the attack.

A key resource for web developers and architects is the Open Web Application Security Project (OWASP). OWASP lists the ten most common web application-related vulnerabilities every year on its website. It also provides advice and tools like WebScarab to help organizations avoid those vulnerabilities.

OWASP Top 10 2010

The OWASP top 10 web application security risks for 2010 are:

1. Injection
2. Cross-site scripting (XSS)
3. Broken authentication and session management
4. Insecure direct object references
5. Cross-site request forgery (CSRF)
6. Security misconfiguration
7. Insecure cryptographic storage
8. Failure to restrict URL access
9. Insufficient transport layer protection
10. Unvalidated redirects and forwards.

Figure 33: OWASP top ten

www.owasp.org/index.php/Top_10_2010

When attacking a web application, there are many attack vectors that a pen tester or attacker can use. The challenge for the administrator is to ensure that each component of the system is protected, hardened and monitored.

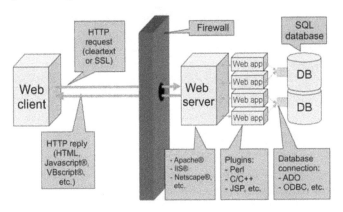

Figure 34: Web application components

Information gathering and discovery

The pen tester begins by learning as much as possible about the configuration and layout of the target system. This includes discovering IP addresses, open ports, operating system fingerprints and files or processes being used by the system.

As seen earlier, this may be accomplished through TCP-connect or TCP-half scanning, NULL scanning and port scans. Information may also be gathered through social engineering attacks.

Exploiting URL mapping

The web application is reached via the URL for the site. The URL guides the process through the various steps necessary to provide the requested service. This URL will include the address, the path, the application, and the database parameters for a database query.

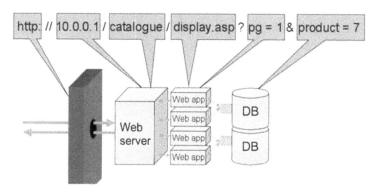

Figure 35: URL structure

Many attackers have been able to reach hidden files or other unauthorized data by manipulating the URL. For example, a recent survey sent out by a company via e-mail provided URLs to click on to fill out the survey to win a prize; however, the surveys were in sequential order and the survey number was in the URL. This allowed anyone to enter in the numbers for other people's surveys and read or alter the survey data – and create multiple entries to the survey for themselves.

URL login hacking

When a person logs into a remote site, the log-in data is often included in the URL sent to the remote server. By manipulating the data in the URL, an attacker may be able to log in as another user (horizontal privilege escalation) or even change their log-in level to a higher level of access (vertical privilege escalation).

User	URL path
Lee	https://site/index.php?id=lee&isadmin=false&menu=basic
Jason	https://site/index.php?id=jason&isadmin=false&menu=basic
Wayne	https://site/index.php?id=wayne&isadmin=true&menu=full

Login as Lee, then change the URL to:
https://site/index.php?id=jason&isadmin=false&menu=basic

If the request is successful, then the application is vulnerable to horizontal privilege escalation.

Figure 36: URL manipulation

Cross-site scripting (XSS)

Cross-site scripting is a common vulnerability of many web applications. It allows an attacker to execute script on a remote victim's machine. By planting a script on a web server – which executes when the victim visits that site – the attacker can gain access to the user session, retrieve data, and monitor the pages viewed by the user.

Unicode and other injection attacks

One of the methods used by attackers is to use alternate forms of data entry to bypass firewall rules or monitoring software. There are many ways to submit the same command to a system. These include Unicode values and other forms of canonicalization. For example, "%c0%af" and "%c1%9c" are the Unicode representations for "/" and "\". With canonicalization, there are many ways to write a filename or command; for example, the command "C:\inetpub\wwwroot\cgibin\..\..\..\Windows\System32\cm d.exe" is really a canonicalization of the real command "C:\Windows\System32\cmd.exe".

Internet Information Services® (IIS®)

Fortunately for attackers, there has always been a wealth of attack vectors and vulnerabilities available. A common platform for web services has been Internet Information Services (IIS) and, like all other platforms, it has been subject to many types of attacks over the years. Each version improves the security over the previous versions and many of the vulnerabilities that led to attacks, such as Slammer, have been patched. The attacking community will usually target the most popular systems; that way, their attack will have the most effect. After all, where is the prestige in attacking a system that only has two users around the world?

Most of the attacks against IIS have been centered on unvalidated and improper input, such as bounds checking and buffer overflows. The primary method of preventing an attack via any platform is to apply the security patches as quickly as possible and harden the systems by turning off unnecessary services.

Case study: Telco

The client organization had a mix of Windows® and UNIX-based systems that they wanted to test. They wanted an in-depth and wide-ranging test – spanning the entire 15,000-employee organization and all its departments and operations. The testing team was creative, determined and not easily discouraged. The first thing they discovered was that the organization had taken extraordinary steps to filter all incoming traffic from the Internet, with thousands of rules on the firewalls and vigorous monitoring of all network traffic. The only problem was that the organization allowed Secure Shell® (SSH®) sessions and, since those were encrypted, the firewalls were ineffective at monitoring and controlling SSH traffic.

The testing team found that the administrators of the Windows® systems were very careful and always kept patches up to date and systems hardened. The Windows® administrators were paranoid of any breach or problem and locked their systems down well.

The problem, however, was with the UNIX systems. The admins there were not as diligent. They knew that their systems were not as vulnerable as the Windows® systems and they became slack in their duties. In a matter of moments, the pen testers had uncovered flaws in the UNIX systems that granted them root access and unlimited control. They discovered the UNIX administrators' passwords and "owned" those systems. Sometimes, it is good to be a little afraid and, therefore, a lot more careful.

The greatest irony of all was that the password used by one of the UNIX administrators was the same password he used for his Windows® system, so when the UNIX systems were broken into, the Windows® systems were also compromised.

Protecting web applications

The most basic rule for protecting a web application is to start with input validation. All input to a web server must be considered untrusted and subject to review. Too often, an attacker is able to modify hidden fields in a form and adjust data that the attacker should not be able to modify – such as the price of a product in an online purchase. The application may check the quantity or data in other fields that the user of an e-commerce website is expected to change, but if the application accepts all the other fields without verifying if they have been changed, then the organization may ship the product to the customer at a fraction of the real price. All input should be validated against a list of allowable values.

The next step in protecting a web application is to use proper architecture. Web servers and other internet-facing services should be located behind a firewall and in an isolated DMZ or extranet.

Error handling is also a problem with many web applications. The error codes provided in the event of a user error are often too verbose and can provide enough information to assist the attacker in refining and launching their attack.

Directory traversal

Directory traversal allows a person to move up levels in a directory and thereby access files at a higher level than they are currently at. For an administrator this is usually necessary, however, users accessing a system remotely should not be able to escalate their privilege levels this way. This attack is usually done by sending the command to move up in the directory stack to the system in a format (Unicode, for example) that eludes the protection from the firewall.

Cookies

Cookies are useful tools to make visiting a website more user-friendly for the user. The cookie stores information about the user and the session that facilitates the interaction between the user and the web server; however, the cookie may contain sensitive information that can be useful for session hijacking or lead to information disclosure. An attacker may also manipulate the cookie using tools like CookieSpy.

Questions

1. Attacks against e-commerce sites are usually achieved by stealing data in:
   a) Storage and processing
   b) Transport and input fields
   c) Output or reports
   d) Storage and transport.

Answer: D

2. One of the greatest challenges to the investigation of computer crime is:
   a) Lack of good forensics tools
   b) Obtaining evidence and gaining co-operation from international sources
   c) Decrease in serious criminal activity
   d) Law enforcement not being willing to pursue incident reports.

Answer: B

3. Improper data can be sneaked through a firewall by:
   a) Encrypting the packets carrying malicious code
   b) Disabling the firewall and altering the rule set
   c) Flooding the firewall with UDP or ICMP packets
   d) Poisoning the ARP table to divert malicious traffic.

Answer: A

4. One open source tool that can be used to test the security of a web application is:
   a) Nmap
   b) hping2
   c) WebScarab
   d) SAINT.

Answer: C

5. A user manipulating their user permissions to appear as another legitimate peer on the system is an example of:
   a) Vertical escalation
   b) Unicode-based URL manipulation
   c) Horizontal escalation

d) SQL injection.

Answer: C

6. A common resource used by an attacker to gain knowledge about a target system is:
   a) DNS poisoning
   b) Error messages
   c) Deletion of ARP tables
   d) Misuse case modeling.

Answer: B

CHAPTER 9: PREPARING THE REPORT

The ultimate goal of penetration testing is to help an organization to secure their networks, systems and databases. The pen tester is given the responsibility of providing meaningful information to the client organization, which will enable them to put forward a plan for mitigating any vulnerabilities and developing enhanced security strategies.

The penetration test report will often include several sections, including a brief summary, a listing of all work done, a detailed list of vulnerabilities found, a ranking of the risk level for each vulnerability, a list of recommendations, and a summary of the tester's opinion on the overall health of the organization's security framework. It is important, however, to remember to separate opinion from facts and findings, and not mix opinion with fact.

Overview

The first part of the report is an overview of the penetration testing project. It includes a description of the scope of the project (what was included in the test and what was determined to be out of scope). It is important to include this, so that the organization does not have the mistaken impression that the test covered areas that were not included in the test program and can schedule more tests to cover those areas not in the original scope. It can also be that the scope of the project changes during the performance of the tests. If a serious vulnerability is found during the test in an area not included in the original scope, then it may have been necessary to re-evaluate the test and make a determination of whether to expand or adjust the scope.

The overview should also detail the authority for the test – who approved it and what regulations, standards or organizational policies applied to the area being tested. This information is especially important when the test has been carried out to satisfy a compliance or audit requirement.

Executive summary

In most cases, the report should include an executive summary that presents a high-level overview of the test, the findings and the recommendations. This summary is prepared for upper management and regulatory bodies, and allows them to gain an overall picture of the test without disclosing or boring them with detailed descriptions of tests, findings and recommendations about configurations, etc. The executive summary of the report must not contain detailed technical descriptions that would only serve to confuse a senior manager and cause them to ignore the recommendations.

Detailed report

The detailed report contains the in-depth description of the test, vulnerabilities and recommendations. It may also contain more opinions from the tester on what the priorities should be, what the associated level of risk is for each vulnerability and a list of various options or potential solutions to resolve the identified security problems. The tester may also recommend where more testing may be needed.

This is where many reports fail to serve the needs of the client organization. The tester and report writers must remember that the primary purpose of the organization is to stay in business. That means that the systems and networks of the organization must serve to support some form of business function. When evaluating the vulnerabilities and providing recommendations on how to address or mitigate those vulnerabilities, the pen tester must not offer solutions that would prevent the system from providing its primary function – to support the business.

Case study: Utility company

The pen testing team had done excellent work and, with great pride, they began the exit interview meeting with the client organization. By following all the best practices of a good pen testing team, they had uncovered some potentially serious issues and were confident of the value they were providing to the client. As each member of the client organization entered the boardroom, they were presented a booklet outlining the scope, results and recommendations of the report. Printed in full color with graphics and notes, it was impressive and authoritative.

Forty-five minutes into the presentation – by which time the lead partner of the testing organization had already outlined the tests and findings, and was well into the list of recommendations – the Vice President of IT for the client organization interrupted with a question. "What business are we in?" he demanded. The leader of the testing team replied, "You are a service organization – a utility."

The Vice President then said, "Yes, but what is the purpose of our network and our systems?"

Discussion ensued, in which it was agreed that the website that was tested was to allow for customers to interact with the client organization and order products, check order statuses, update their profiles, and check their payment histories.

"So, now that we know the business context of this system, let's look at the recommendations you are giving us," suggested the Vice President. "If I was to adopt these last few recommendations you have just suggested, would I still be able to support our business?"

The answer was, predictably, "No." The pen testing team had just provided an excellent report that, in effect, would put the organization out of business. Such reports have little or no value to the client and result in the credibility of the pen testing team being damaged. A report that has good and poor recommendations is likely to be discarded. In fact, this report had several good recommendations that were then ignored, since the testing team had forgotten the most important directive of all: "Do not put the client out of business."

Working papers and evidence

A pen testing report should be authoritative and factual. It must not be based on opinion or a generic standard that is not aligned to the business of the organization. Far too many pen tests are done clinically – without regard to the culture or operational environment of the client – and far too many tests are done haphazardly and with a lack of a clear, thorough methodology, which would ensure that everything is done according to the defined scope of the project.

Just as a scientist would do for a scientific hypothesis, the pen tester must first define the tests according to what needs to be proved, what a pass or fail standard would be, how the test will be conducted and what information the tests must provide. Once the test has been completed, there should be tangible evidence of what tests were conducted and what the results were. This leads to the analysis and interpretation of the results and then the determination of the recommendations for what needs to be corrected. Each recommendation in the report must be backed up by factual work papers and evidence that ensures the recommendation is valid and credible.

Determining risk levels

As seen earlier, the risk level is the likelihood of an adverse event affecting the ability of the business to meet its mission and objectives. However, risk can also be measured in terms of the amount of impact it could have. Would the entire organization be affected, or only one department? Would sensitive data potentially be disclosed, or only low-value information? Would the damage be tangible (quantitative – money, for example) or intangible (qualitative: reputation or morale)? The pen tester must be able to determine the level of risk associated with any finding in the report, so that the client organization will know how to prioritize and schedule their mitigation strategy. No organization will ever have enough money or resources (time and skilled manpower) to mitigate all risk immediately; setting out priorities is important, so that the most serious issues are addressed before the less serious, and so that the minor issues are not ignored for so long that they become major problems.

Risk response

The primary options for addressing the risk an organization is facing are quite straightforward. You can reduce (mitigate), accept, avoid or transfer the risk. The organization has to balance cost against benefit to know what the best strategy to take is.

Risk acceptance

Risk acceptance is knowingly and consciously agreeing that the organization is comfortable with the level of risk being faced. A person that loans a book or tool to a friend knows that there is a risk that the item may not be returned. They may attempt to mitigate the risk of loss by putting their name on it, or cautioning the friend to be sure to return it, but, regardless of the precautions they take, there is still the chance that the item (the asset) will be lost. The lender accepts this risk; they may be reluctant, but, in the end, they have a risk threshold or risk appetite that allows them to lend the item knowing that a loss may occur. If they were to not loan the item – being quite convinced that it would never be returned – they are practicing risk avoidance.

Organizations realize that not all risk can be mitigated or avoided, especially as the cost of mitigating the risk for a given incident may be higher than the impact of the incident itself. The level of risk that the organization is willing to accept is known as their "risk appetite" or "acceptable risk level." A pen tester should never recommend a solution for a vulnerability that would be more costly to the organization than the cost of the impact if the problem were to occur.

Risk avoidance

Risk avoidance is avoiding a situation that may present an unacceptable level of risk to the organization. Part of a feasibility study and strategic plan is determining which initiatives the organization is willing to pursue and which ones should be avoided due to the risk of losing money being too high. In considering whether to enhance their website by adding in new functionality, an organization must practice risk avoidance and consider whether adding that functionality into their systems would pose a level of risk that is above the risk appetite of the organization. If the risk is too high, and the cost to mitigate it too severe, the organization may simply choose to avoid that risk by not adding in the new service or functionality.

Risk transference

Most organizations will purchase insurance as protection from catastrophic loss. The loss of a building or major asset may result in the financial collapse of the organization. Therefore, they purchase insurance to cover a portion of the costs associated with that loss in the event that it does occur. By purchasing insurance, they have transferred a portion of their risk to a third party – the insurance company.

Risk mitigation (reduction)

It could be stated that the primary purpose of a penetration test is to mitigate risk. The pen test finds vulnerabilities, determines the risk level associated with those vulnerabilities and provides the client organization with a set of recommendations for how they could reduce those vulnerabilities to an acceptable level.

Risk is reduced through the implementation of controls – technical, physical, administrative and operational controls. However, each control has a cost. The control may cost something to implement or to operate, and it may impact productivity, reduce functionality, or affect employee morale. Determining the correct response to a risk – which involves considering what is an acceptable level of risk and what is the cost versus the benefit of the control method – is the science of risk mitigation.

An example of deploying risk mitigation is the protection of a building. The owner wants to protect the building from break-ins and will deploy a series of controls to deter, prevent, detect and respond to break-ins. However, some buildings require more protection than others. It may not make sense to deploy expensive and complicated controls to protect a building that does not contain valuable assets, but it would be inappropriate not to deploy expensive controls to protect a building containing high value items – such as a bank or military installation. A pen tester must be careful not to recommend controls that would cost more to implement and maintain than the building is worth!

In some cases, the pen tester may identify a critical vulnerability during the test that requires immediate mitigation. When the pen tester finds a critical issue, they should notify management immediately, so that the problem can be addressed promptly. In this case, the issue should still be included in the penetration test report, but noted as having been fixed. This ensures that there is a record of the vulnerability and later tests can ensure that the vulnerability continues to be mitigated.

Residual risk

Residual risk is the risk that remains after the controls have been implemented. Risk cannot be totally eliminated, but it should be reduced to a level that is acceptable to the organization. Residual risk must be equal to or less than the acceptable risk. In the case where an organization is willing to self-insure for all risks that would cost less than one million dollars, the cost of many incidents or risks is going to be less than that risk acceptance threshold of one million dollars. Therefore, the residual risk or actual risk is less than an acceptable risk level.

Risk in the penetration test report

The pen tester should be able to provide the client organization with an assessment of their current level of risk and the risk levels associated with each vulnerability identified in the report. Since risk is always evolving as new technologies, vulnerabilities and threats emerge, and as the organization changes its operations or processes, risk management is a continuous process. A pen test is a picture of risk at a point in time, and should be repeated on a regular basis.

Audit risk

No penetration test is perfect, and there will always be a risk that a serious vulnerability in the client organization will not have been identified or included in the report. This is known as the audit risk. The pen tester should take precautions to avoid missing vulnerabilities by following methodologies, standards and best practices. However, every report should have a caveat that protects the pen tester from being held accountable for errors or omissions, and makes sure that they are not put in a position of being culpable if a subsequent attack exploits a vulnerability that had been missed.

Report confidentiality

A penetration testing report is an extremely confidential document and the pen testing organization must observe appropriate precautions in the preparation, delivery and storage of it.

Only personnel that have a need to know and have signed non-disclosure agreements should be able to access the report or any files or test results associated with the test. It is important to consider this in the printing of the report. There have been cases where a pen test for an organization has been released by employees of a company contracted to print the report. There have also been instances where copies of the report were found in the trash or recycling bins of the pen testing or printing company. This is especially likely to happen when draft copies of the report or the first print copy is discarded.

The report should be password protected and all extra copies should be shredded. The pen testing company may need to keep a copy of the report and test results (in case of future litigation or contests of the report), but it must be kept in a secure manner and a digital signature for the report must be generated. If the pen testing company is required to destroy all copies of the report upon delivery to the client, then they must have a sign-off and release from the client organization upon delivery.

Delivering the report

The penetration testing report should be delivered to the authorized personnel of the client organization. It is best to do this via a face-to-face meeting. A meeting should be arranged with appropriate personnel, so that the report can be presented to the client and the client has the opportunity to question or discuss the content of the report with the testing team.

The penetration tester should offer a clear and concise summary of the contents of the report, highlighting the important points and providing an overview of the recommendations and general state of the security of the client organization. Having graphs, tables and charts in the presentation and final report may help the client (especially senior management) understand the content of the report.

Prior to delivering the report, it may be advisable to have a meeting with the client's IT department and other departments to gain a consensus on the recommendations contained in the report and ensure that the statements in the report regarding the client organization are accurate and acceptable.

Key learning points

- The report must be accurate, thorough, complete and credible.
- The report should be free from technical jargon and the use of terminology that may be easily misunderstood.
- Opinions must be separated from fact in the report.
- The report should have a standard layout, with an executive summary, detailed report and supporting evidence.

- The report should list the vulnerabilities, the relative risk of the vulnerabilities, and the recommendations to remediate the vulnerabilities.
- The report should be delivered in a face-to-face meeting with the client organization.
- The confidentiality of the report must be maintained at all times.

Questions

1. What is the purpose of the executive summary of the penetration testing report?
   a) To provide detailed data on vulnerabilities and recommendations for the client organization
   b) To define the schedule to fix any serious vulnerabilities
   c) To provide a high-level overview of the penetration test
   d) To gain consent from senior management to implement the recommendations of the report.

Answer: C

2. One of the primary elements of the pen testing report should be:
   a) Work papers
   b) Statement of scope
   c) Test results
   d) Risk mitigation.

Answer: B

3. All personnel accessing pen testing reports should be:

a) Bound by non-compete agreements
b) Subject to non-disclosure requirements
c) Employees of the client organization
d) Managers or IT staff only.

Answer: B

4. Quantitative risk analysis is based on:
   a) Financial considerations
   b) Scenarios
   c) Cost-benefit analysis
   d) Risk avoidance.

Answer: A

5. Risk mitigation options may include:
   a) Technical controls
   b) Risk assessment
   c) Qualitative risk review
   d) Risk acceptance levels.

Answer: A

APPENDIX 1: LINUX

A discussion on hacking and penetration testing would not be complete without a brief discussion of Linux. Linux is a favorite operating system of hackers and pen testers due to its flexibility and functionality.

Linux was initially developed by a Finnish schoolboy, Linus Benedict Torvalds, as a way to manage memory on his 386 PC. Linus developed an operating kernel that he then offered to the world as open source code, so that anyone else that wanted to could contribute to its development.

There are many advantages to an open source project, such as Linux, as it can be developed and enhanced using the ingenuity and skills of many people, and any flaws or problems that are found in the program are likely to be found and repaired rapidly. There are no secrets in an open source program!

However, there are also disadvantages to open source software: it is easier to attack, since its flaws and wrinkles are visible to everyone, and not all updates to the code can be immediately trusted.

The Linux shell provides the command line from which many user commands can be executed. By setting up a shell script, a user can execute a series of individual commands. Linux allows the user to customize their system through the use of shells and the option to set individual variables.

The option to run privileged programs on the system is usually restricted to an account at root-level access.

Passwords are kept in a file named "etc/passwd." This file is accessed by many tools and may be a security risk. A more secure place to store passwords is in the shadow file, which stores the passwords in an encrypted format and is not accessible to anyone without root-level access.

There are many tools used in pen testing based on Linux. Having a Linux CD that will allow an administrator to boot up a system from a USB stick or CD will allow an administrator to bypass many Windows® controls and run tools on the system. This can be a valuable way to examine and access a system, scan for malware and even reset Windows® passwords.

The pen tester should become familiar with many of the commands and tools used on UNIX-based systems.

APPENDIX 2: ENCRYPTION

Concepts of cryptography

Cryptography is the art and science of transmitting and storing data in a format that cannot be understood by an unauthorized party. Cryptography has been a key part of secrecy used by the military, governments and tradesmen for thousands of years. Evidence of this can be seen in some of the early samples of encrypted writing used to protect intellectual property in ancient Mesopotamia.

Cryptography is used today for more than just secrecy. Modern cryptography leverages the additional benefits provided by public key or asymmetric cryptographic systems for secrecy, integrity, access control, non-repudiation and authentication.

The following is a very high-level overview of cryptography intended to provide the pen tester with an understanding of the basics.

The definitions and operations of cryptography

Cryptography is the altering of a message into a format in a way that protects it from unauthorized disclosure or modification. The original message in its unaltered format can be called cleartext or plaintext. In this format, it is unprotected and, therefore, readable or understandable to virtually anyone that has access to it.

The alteration of the message is performed by a cryptosystem that will transform the plaintext into ciphertext or a cryptogram. This process is known as encryption. The alteration is performed according to some mathematical operation known as an algorithm. Each person that uses the cryptosystem can select their own secret value – the key or cryptovariable (similar to a password) needed to govern the operation of the algorithm and make the encrypted message unreadable to anyone that does not have the proper key. In this way, many people can use the same algorithm and cryptosystem and still know that other people cannot read their encrypted messages. The secret to cryptography is the protection of the key and making sure that unauthorized people are not able to gain access to the key, and, therefore, be able to decrypt the encrypted message.

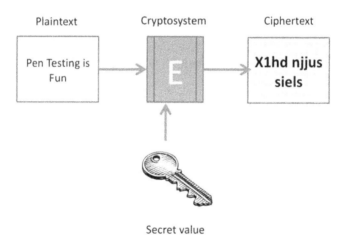

Figure 37: Basic encryption

The two most common operations performed by the cryptosystem are substitution or transposition of the data in the message. Substitution is where the value of one letter in the plaintext is exchanged for another letter – for example, the letter "A" in the plaintext is substituted for the letter "D.[19]"

Transposition is where the same letters are kept in the plaintext, but they are put in a different order. The word "exam" may then be written as "aemx."

Even the most modern cryptosystems rely on substitution and transposition.

Symmetric algorithms

Symmetric algorithms use the same key for both the encryption and decryption of a message. If a message is encrypted with a key value of "19748652," for example, then the same key must be used to decrypt the message. Anyone that had that key would be able to decrypt the encrypted message, so the protection of the key is of primary importance.

Symmetric algorithms are relatively fast and provide high levels of confidentiality. Some of the most commonly used symmetric algorithms include the Advanced Encryption Standard (AES), the older Data Encryption Standard (DES), RC4 (a stream-based cipher used in WEP and WPA), and MARS.®

The disadvantages of symmetric algorithms are scalability and key management. For two people to exchange encrypted messages, they must share the same key. For each pair of people that want to exchange messages, a different key is needed. The more people that want to

---

[19] The Caesar cipher operated in this manner – merely substituting the letter in the plaintext with the letter three places over in the alphabet. "A" would, therefore, become "D"; "B" would become "E", etc.

exchange messages, the more keys are needed; this can become an administrative challenge. All of those keys must be protected, stored and transmitted securely to each party in the data exchange.

Asymmetric algorithms

In the mid 70s, the world became aware of a new method of encryption known as asymmetric or public key encryption. Instead of using one shared key to both encrypt and decrypt a message – like symmetric key encryption does – asymmetric encryption uses a key pair. The keys always work in a pair where, if one half of the key pair is used to encrypt a message, the other half of the key pair must be used to decrypt the ciphertext of the message.

The key pair is comprised of two key halves. One half is the private key, which is owned and used *only* by the owner of the key pair. The other half of the key pair is known as the public, and can be shared with everyone and anyone. If Bob owns the key pair, he can encrypt a message with his private key. The only key that can open that message is Bob's public key. To the recipient of the encrypted message, this provides proof of origin. They know, since they can open the encrypted message with Bob's public key, the message *must* have come from Bob. This is known as non-repudiation or proof of origin. A message encrypted with a private key is known as a "signed" message. Since it can be said that the owner has "signed" the message, it can be proven who sent the message. A message encrypted with a private key can be decrypted by anyone with the public key. As a result, it is not really confidential – but at least it is known who sent it.

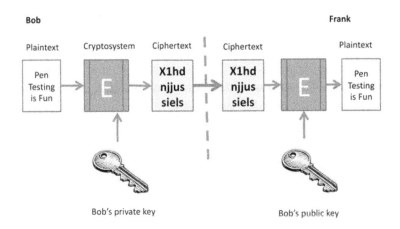

Figure 38: Proof of origin

If Frank wants to send a message to Bob confidentially, he will just encrypt the message with Bob's public key. Since Bob's private key is the only key that is able to open a message encrypted with Bob's public key, Frank knows that only Bob will be able to decrypt and read the encrypted message.

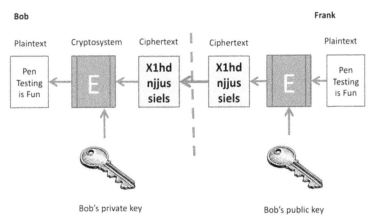

Figure 39: Confidentiality

Certificates

One of the challenges of public key cryptography is proving that Frank truly has Bob's public key, and that he has not been sent an imposter's public key instead. This could happen in the case of a man-in-the-middle attack, where an attacker has managed to place themselves into the middle of the key exchange process. One way to prevent this is through the use of certificates. A certificate is issued by a certificate authority (CA). The CA issues a certificate following the X.509 standard that attests to the correct ownership of a public key. When Frank receives a certificate from a trusted CA, he is confident that the public key that is in the certificate belongs to the owner of the certificate.

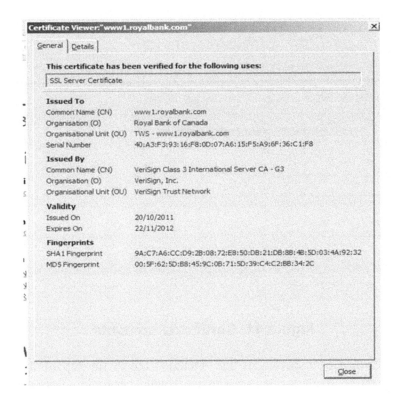

Figure 40: Certificates

This example shows the public key certificate issued by VeriSign (one of the best-known CAs) to the Royal Bank of Canada (RBC). As can be seen, this is a Class 3 certificate – which means it has met stringent rules for registration and issuance, so that the client knows the certificate is genuine and associated with the Royal Bank. The example also shows that the certificate has not expired, so it is still valid (unless placed on a certificate revocation list – but that is a discussion for another time).

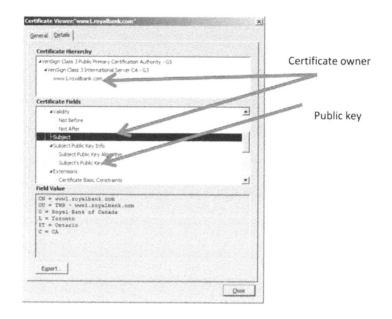

Figure 41: Certificate contents

When a user clicks on the "Details" tab at the top of the certificate, they can see the certificate contents. As seen here, the certificate contains the name of the subject – the owner (in this case the Royal Bank) – and the public key of the owner. Clicking on the public key field would display the 2048 bit RSA® public key of the Royal Bank. Now that the user has the public key of the bank, they can encrypt data with that public key and send it to the bank, knowing that no one else can read or alter their message, since only the Royal Bank would have the correct private key needed to open the encrypted message.

Characteristics of asymmetric algorithms

Asymmetric algorithms, such as RSA and Elliptic Curve Cryptography (ECC), are powerful and useful tools in today's world of network encryption and e-commerce. A user anywhere in the world can communicate securely with a company or government agency by using the public key of the company or agency to encrypt the message they want to send. The key management problem symmetric algorithms have of needing a separate key for every pair of users is solved. One public key is enough for everyone to communicate securely with an entity. If a user "signs" a message with their private key, then the receiving party also knows who sent the message (a benefit known as non-repudiation).

However, there is a problem. Asymmetric algorithms require intense amounts of processing power and time. They are very slow compared with symmetric algorithms, and it would be unfeasible to use an asymmetric algorithm, such as RSA, to encrypt a large message. It would simply take too long to encrypt and decrypt (perhaps even days!)

Hybrid systems

The challenges of asymmetric algorithms being too slow to use effectively, and of managing all the key pairs required to use symmetric algorithms are overcome through the use of a hybrid system.

A hybrid system uses asymmetric algorithms to solve symmetric algorithms' problem of key management, and employs the speed of symmetric algorithms for bulk message encryption.

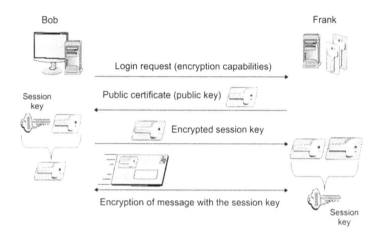

Figure 42: SSL

In a hybrid system, the originator of a message (Bob) can encrypt the message using a symmetric algorithm (such as AES). This provides fast encryption and very good levels of confidentiality.

Using the public key of the receiver (Frank), Bob can send the AES key used to encrypt the message to Frank by encrypting the AES key with Frank's public key.

As seen from the diagram, SSL is an implementation of a hybrid system. Bob sends a message to Frank to say that he would like a secure log-in to his web server. Frank replies with his public key certificate, so that Bob knows he is using Frank's public key – not that of an imposter pretending to be Frank. Bob can encrypt the AES key he will use for this log-in session (hence the use of the name "session key" for this AES key) with Frank's public key. Even though public key algorithms are slow, the AES key is very short and will not take much time to encrypt and decrypt.

Now both Bob and Frank have the session key they require, they can communicate securely over an untrusted network. This is the process used for many Internet services, such as online banking and shopping. Most virtual private networks (VPNs) also use this type of hybrid encryption to set up a secure encrypted tunnel for two parties to communicate over.

Message integrity

When two parties are communicating, there is always the risk that the message will not be received correctly at the far end. Especially when communicating over a noisy or insecure network, the message may be altered by noise or the intentional actions of an attacker as it moves from one point to another. This is why message integrity checks are so important. When conducting e-commerce, a store needs to know exactly how many products to ship and where to ship them to. A bit of noise in the network may change the data and result in the wrong products being shipped to the wrong places.

Early forms of integrity checks were carried out through parity bits, checksums and check digits, but those can all be altered by an attacker using a man-in-the-middle attack.

Hashing

In order to ensure the integrity of a message today, hash functions are used. It will be easier to understand this topic if you remember that hash functions are for integrity – not for encryption. The user of a hashing algorithm, such as MD5® or SHA-1 (or the other SHA variants), will run the message through the hashing algorithm to generate a digest or hash of the message. The hash is simply a small value (in the case of MD5, 128 bits in length) that serves as a fingerprint or representation of the message. A hash is extremely accurate; if one bit of the source message was to be changed, then at least 40% of the hash of that message would be different. In this way, the users of the hash are confident that, if the hash of a message that is received by the receiver is the same as the hash value sent by the originator of the message, then the received message is an exact copy of the original message.

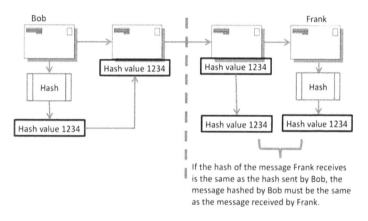

Figure 43: Hash functions

Digital signatures

Earlier in this chapter, it was noted that an advantage of asymmetric algorithms was that they could prove who sent a message and establish the principle of non-repudiation. To repudiate is to deny, so non-repudiation is to have a way to prevent a person from being able to deny something. This is a serious concern in e-commerce, as a person may later want to claim that they were not the person that ordered a product or told a stockbroker to sell their shares. We saw that if a message was "signed" with a private key, the receiver would know who the originator of the message was (since they could validate the signature with the public key of the originator). But we also saw that encrypting or signing a large message with asymmetric algorithms could require days to decrypt it, so that is not a feasible solution.

In the paragraph on hashing, we saw that a hash was a small fingerprint of a message that could prove the integrity of the message. So, what happens when we combine hashing with signing? We get a digital signature. A digital signature proves the source (non-repudiation) of the message, as well as the integrity of the message (demonstrating it has not been altered). Remember that a digital signature is not the same as a digitized signature – a digitized signature is just the scan of your autograph.

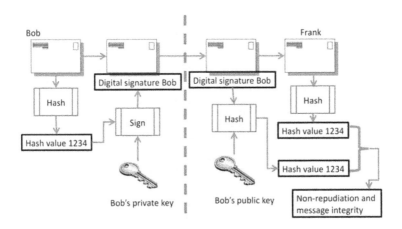

Figure 44: Digital signatures

As seen in the diagram, a digital signature is created by encrypting (signing) a hash of the message with the private key of the sender (Bob). The digital signature is then appended to the source message and sent, along with the message, to the receiver (Frank). Please note that the message was sent unencrypted in this example – a digital signature may be used with the encryption of the message, but this is not mandatory. The Digital Signature Standard (DSS) does not address the confidentiality of the message – just the source and integrity of it.

When the receiver (Frank) receives the message and the digital signature from Bob, he will validate the digital signature by opening the signature with Bob's public key. Then, he will generate his own hash of the received message and ensure that the hash he creates is the same as the hash signed by Bob.

Uses of cryptography

Cryptography has many uses today: for passwords, VPNs, secure e-commerce, and storage and transmission of sensitive information, for example. Cryptography provides many benefits for organizations, but it must be used carefully, and implemented correctly. The pen tester should test the security of the cryptographic implementation and ensure that keys are chosen properly and protected from compromise.

Some of the risks associated with cryptography are also in the way that an encrypted packet may avoid scrutiny from firewalls and intrusion detection systems. Attackers have also held an organization hostage by encrypting the files of the organization and only selling the encryption key back to the organization at a price. Employees can also hide their actions by encrypting files and communications.

There are many ways to attack cryptographic implementations, but the easiest way is always through social engineering or by taking advantage of errors by employees or administrators.

APPENDIX 3: REGULATIONS AND LEGISLATION

The pen tester may be required to provide the client organization with a proof of compliance with certain legislation, regulations, best practices, or industry standards as a part of the pen testing effort. These regulations vary widely from one jurisdiction to another – from country to country and, often, from state to state.

Many regulations are industry-specific – such as legislation concerning health care – and only apply to that industry sector or vertical. Other legislation applies across all industries in a region or country and are, therefore, horizontal in nature.

A multinational organization may find it nearly impossible to be compliant with the regulations in all the countries they operate in. In fact, since regulations in one country may be in conflict with the regulations from another, it may actually be impossible for the organization to be compliant with the laws of each country.

Figure 45: Compliance and regulations

Examples of regulations and legislation

There are many laws and regulations that a pen tester should be familiar with, including laws on hacking, testing, privacy, financial soundness and protection of nations, organizations and individuals.

Hacking and pen testing

When is a pen test actually an attack and not just a test? One can claim that a test is not conducted with the intent to do damage, but, if the tester is negligent in performing the test and does impact the business of the client, or perhaps even the business of another organization that is affected by the test, is it then an attack? Where is the boundary between probing a network and attacking it? Is a port scan an attack, a precursor to an attack, or just an assessment of the security controls?

The problem is that the answer may be different depending on where you are and what laws apply. In some countries, the possession of testing tools may be seen as a criminal act – even by legitimate testing organizations. In other countries, there are few or no laws – and, without a foundation of laws, it may be impossible to deter unwanted behavior.

Privacy

Privacy legislation is one of the most high-profile types of legislation today. Many countries are passing privacy legislation to protect personally identifiable information (PII), such as addresses, locations, financial data, or health information.

A major consideration regarding privacy is trans-border data flow: what information is permitted to be moved from one country to another? In a world of Cloud Computing this becomes all the more challenging.

Some examples of privacy legislation include the European Union Principles on Privacy. The core principles are:

1. The reason for gathering of data must be specified at the time of collection.
2. Data cannot be used for other purposes.
3. Unnecessary data should not be collected.
4. Data should only be kept for as long as it is needed to accomplish the stated task.
5. Only the necessary individuals who are required to accomplish the stated task should be allowed access to the data.
6. Whoever is responsible for securely storing the data should not allow unintentional "leaking" of data.

US laws include the Health Insurance Portability and Accountability Act (HIPAA); Electronic Communications Privacy Act, the e-Government act of 2002.

Employee privacy

Is it legal to monitor an employee's e-mail or other internet activity? Can a pen tester observe what an employee is doing, what can they do if they observe something against company policy? What should be done if a test reveals illegal activity? These are all questions that must be addressed prior to the start of any test or examination of a network or system.

Non-disclosure agreements

Any person working on a pen test or in a security function should be trustworthy and honest. Ensuring this may require a background check and security clearance before employment, and follow-up review on an annual basis during employment. The employee should be required to sign and observe the conditions of a non-disclosure agreement, and be bonded to preserve the confidentiality of client information – even following employment or the termination of the services contract.

Some pen testing and security companies may even prevent an employee, that has worked on the systems for one client, from working on contracts for other clients in the same industry, in order to prevent information leakage between competitors.

Access controls

All access to pen tests, client data and other protected information must be on a strictly "need to know" basis and with enforcement of "least privilege." Operating on a "need to know" basis prevents any person from accessing any data that they do not directly need to access as a part of their job function. The practice of "least privilege" enforces authorization controls that will only let a user perform limited operations on the data they can access – such as read-only, write-only, create, delete, etc. This prevents an individual that only needs to have read access to the data from making an accidental or intentional change.

Financial legislation

Some examples of legislation regarding financial operations are the Gramm-Leach-Bliley Act of 1999, Sarbanes-Oxley Act (SOX 404), and Basel II. There are also numerous standards, such as the Generally Accepted Accounting Practices (GAAP), although these may also differ from country to country.

Standards

The use of a standard or recognized best practice may guide the performance of a penetration test. Some standards include the ISO27002 published by the International Organization for Standardization; the Payment Card Industry Data Security Standard (PCI DSS) and its related payment application standards; COBIT; NIST and ITIL.®

Appendix 3: Regulations and Legislation

The PCI DSS standards are an excellent set of standards for designing and operating a secure system. Its core requirements are:

1. Install and maintain a firewall configuration to protect cardholder data.

2. Do not use vendor-supplied defaults for system passwords and other security parameters.

3. Protect stored cardholder data.

4. Encrypt transmission of cardholder data across open, public networks. [WEP cannot be used.]

5. Use and regularly update anti-virus software or programs.

6. Develop and maintain secure systems and applications.

7. Restrict access to cardholder data by business need to know.

8. Assign a unique ID to each person with computer access.

9. Restrict physical access to cardholder data.

10. Track and monitor all access to network resources and cardholder data.

11. Regularly test security systems and processes.

    [Requirement 11.3 clarifies this to explicitly mandate internal *and* external penetration testing of networks *and* applications.]

12. Maintain a policy that addresses information security for all personnel.[20]

---

[20] *www.pcisecuritystandards.org/security_standards/index.php*.

Protection of intellectual property

One of the most important assets an organization has is its intellectual property – its patents, copyrights, trademarks and trade secrets. These elements of intellectual property (IP) must be protected, since they are, in effect, the competitive distinction and value that makes the organization competitive and profitable, and protects their market share. If the patents are lost, trade secrets are compromised or trademarks are violated, then the organization may have no way to compete effectively against lower-priced competition. Think of a pharmaceutical company that has spent years researching a new drug. If the data about that drug was to be acquired by a competitor, then the original company would have no way to recover its investment in research and would, possibly, face financial ruin. For this reason, the pen tester must be especially diligent to ensure that an organization's IP is adequately protected and not subject to compromise.

APPENDIX 4: INCIDENT MANAGEMENT

Concepts of incident management

Incident management is the practice of preparing for, preventing, detecting, reacting to and recovering from adverse events when they impact business operations, and then documenting lessons to be learned for the future.

The lessons learned from an incident may be valuable in protecting the organization from future incidents and enabling it to respond faster and more accurately, and minimizing the impact of the crisis. However, we see that many organizations do not learn from incidents; instead, they seem to rather hide or move on – avoiding the pain of examining what the conditions were that led up to the crisis. This approach may cause the organization to remain vulnerable to the same problem again and, in fact, it may lead to a much more serious crisis occurring the next time.

The following is not an in-depth review of the entire incident management process, but it does outline some of the key steps for a penetration testing team to take to be prepared for an incident that occurs during their testing.

Incident preparation

Being prepared for an incident is facing the reality that sometimes, despite the best efforts of the organization, things can go wrong. Preparing starts with determining who has the leadership role in a crisis (who "owns" the incident and has the authority to manage the response by allocating resources, incurring costs, and reporting on the crisis). The leader must be provided with the skilled resources – tools and personnel – needed to manage a crisis, should one occur. The personnel must be trained according to the skills they may require.

In the case of pen testing, the testing team must be prepared, in case anything goes wrong during the tests, and also know what to do if they encounter a crisis during the test.

A common challenge that arises in nearly every crisis is that of communication. How will critical personnel be reached? How can a rumor be controlled (especially in the world of social media, where anyone can post anything online in a matter of seconds)? And how can it be ensured that management is kept informed of the crisis, and employees, business partners and customers are provided with accurate information?

The secret to resolving most incidents is preparation – the more time spent on preparation, the more manageable an incident will be.

Incident detection

Incident detection is the skill and practice of knowing what is going on – being alerted to an incident, making the initial decisions as to the scope, source and severity of the incident, and initialing the response teams.

The initial stages of dealing with an incident include triage, containment and escalation of the problem. Once an alert has indicated a potential incident, the response team must determine whether the incident is truly a problem, or a just a false alarm. Once the incident has been confirmed, the first step is to stop it from spreading and contain it as effectively as possible. The less damage caused, the less there will be to repair later.

Perhaps the most important feature of this step is the documentation of the incident. No one can be expected to remember the sequence of events and details of an event following the resolution of the incident. For this reason, it is important to begin creating a record of the incident as soon as possible. This will provide the data needed for the subsequent review, learning and analysis of the incident.

Incident response

Depending on the scope, nature and extent of the incident, the appropriate personnel will need to be engaged and begin the process of responding to – and recovering from – the incident. The primary objective of this phase is to get the business back to a normal state of operations as quickly as possible. In the case of a problem caused by the pen test, the team must be able to contact the key personnel of the client organization and have the knowledge and skills needed to rebuild, stabilize and re-initiate system operations.

In some cases, the response will also require the preservation of evidence. Especially if any criminal activity is involved, the seizure of any evidence must be done with regard to the appropriate standards for handling, documenting, protection, and transportation of evidence. The evidence must be collected in a lawful manner and be as accurate and authentic as possible. The evidence must be documented in a "chain of custody" that details the actions taken with regard to the evidence at all times during its life cycle. There must be an unbroken chain of record for who, what, when, where, and how the evidence was handled at all times.

Follow-up

Following every incident, a follow-up meeting should be held with all involved parties to review the incident and seek out any lessons that could be learned from it. Almost every incident is the result of a series of events that happened in a critical order and, if an organization can learn how to avoid any of the events that led up to the incident, they may prevent similar incidents in the future. Lessons learned may indicate the need for more training, better tools, better monitoring, faster responses, or new or enhanced technical or administrative controls.

ADDITIONAL QUESTIONS AND ANSWERS

1. Why wouldn't it be surprising to find Netcat on a Trojaned computer?
   a) Netcat can be used to block any port from proper operation.
   b) Netcat is used by system administrators to detect remote access Trojans.
   c) Netcat can be used to perform port scanning.
   d) Netcat encrypts all communications.

2. Why is tunneling-based Trojan software so useful for hackers if it is installed inside a corporate network?
   a) Tunneling software uses ports that are not well known, e.g. 12345.
   b) Stateful inspection firewalls can only filter server ports of 1-1023.
   c) It makes network penetration trivial – the tunneling occurs using whichever port(s) the firewall is configured to allow.
   d) Anti-Trojan software does not have signatures for tunneling Trojans and, therefore, it is easy for end-users to install tunneling Trojans.

3. What technology has made Trojans easy to distribute?
   a) Digitally signed software
   b) Legacy assembly language code
   c) Personal firewall software
   d) EXE wrappers.

4. What built-in Windows® command can be used to help find remote-access Trojans?
   a) Netstat -a
   b) Ipconfig /displaydns
   c) Nbtstat -c
   d) Netdiag.

5. Which of the following ports is most frequently associated with a Trojan on a Windows® computer?
   a) 53
   b) 135
   c) 3389
   d) 31337.

6. What type of software is used by an administrator to detect modified files or executables (system or otherwise) by comparing the new hash to the hash on the original, trusted file?
   a) AES
   b) WPA2
   c) Traceroute
   d) Integrity checkers.

7. What sniffer program is capable of reconstructing associated TCP packets into a session showing application layer data from the client to the server and vice-versa?
   a) Packetyzer
   b) EtherApe®
   c) Wireshark
   d) Arpwatch.

8. The process of flooding a local segment with thousands of random MAC addresses can result in some switches behaving like a hub. What is the goal of the hacker?
   a) Denial of service
   b) ARP cache poisoning
   c) Sniffing in a switched network
   d) SYN flood.

9. What process does a Cisco switch use to prevent or detect ARP cache poisoning?
   a) ARP watch
   b) Dynamic ARP inspection
   c) VLANs
   d) IPSec-ready.

10. Which of the following protocols send data in cleartext, and is thus insecure?
    a) SSH
    b) SNMPv3
    c) POP3
    d) WEP.

11. What technology can be deployed at the network layer to protect against sniffing?
    a) SSL
    b) Certificates
    c) IPsec
    d) SSH.

12. Which protocol contains encrypted versions of telnet, file transfer protocol (FTP), and file copy for both Linux and Windows® computers?
    a) SSL
    b) Open SSH
    c) IEEE 802.1X
    d) SPF.

13. What technologies could a company deploy to protect all data passing from an employee's home computer to the corporate intranet?
    a) IPsec
    b) DNSSEC
    c) WEP
    d) IKE.

14. By spoofing an IP address and inserting the attacker's MAC address into an unsolicited ARP reply packet, an attacker is performing what kind of attack?
    a) Denial of service
    b) Sniffing in a switched network via ARP poisoning
    c) ARP flood
    d) Birthday.

15. Why is passive sniffing much harder to detect than active sniffing (if not impossible)?
    a) Passive sniffing injects fewer packets into the switch.
    b) Passive sniffing can be done only via software – not via hardware.
    c) A device that only receives packets is undetectable.

d) Active sniffing requires a unique signature to log network data.

16. What hashed authentication credentials can be sniffed and possibly cracked offline (assuming time is not an issue)?
   a) SHA-1
   b) Diffie-Hellman
   c) Kerberos®
   d) EAP-TLS.

17. A direct attack on a database system is one that attacks what?
   a) The application code of the database system
   b) The data residing on the database tables
   c) The web front-end to the database
   d) The first user account created on the database server.

18. Which of the following options most closely represents a typical format for a Microsoft SQL injection script?
   a) ' OR 'a'='a
   b) AND 1=1
   c) ' OR 1=1; - -
   d) '; SELECT * FROM *.

19. What is one way an attacker can determine if a database front-end application is vulnerable to SQL injection?
   a) Entering a single star (*) in the username field
   b) Checking all outgoing TCP connections after browsing the web application

   c) Just attempting an attack (there is no way to check)
   d) Entering a single quotation mark (') in the password field.

20. SQL injection is defined as:
   a) The gaining of access to a database management system by injecting code into a system process.
   b) The insertion of invalidated SQL code into an input field, which is used to directly build an SQL statement.
   c) The process of placing new data into a database by inserting malicious code.
   d) Altering data on a victim's database server to that of a hacker's choice.

21. Which of the following SQL scripts will cause the SQL server to cease operations?
   a) '; NET STOP SQLSERVER –
   b) ' OR 1=1; CLOSE WITHNOWAIT;
   c) '; NET STOP SQLSERVERAGENT—
   d) '; SHUTDOWN WITH NOWAIT; --.

22. When conducting a TCP scan for SQL servers on a given network address range, which port is being interrogated?
   a) 443
   b) 1334
   c) 1433
   d) 433.

23. Which ports should be blocked on the perimeter and internal firewall to best protect the Microsoft SQL database server from unauthorized inbound connections?
    a) 1433, 1434
    b) 443, 434
    c) 1443, 1444
    d) 80, 139.

24. Types of potential vulnerabilities that are commonly scanned for using a rainbow table include:
    a) Password vulnerabilities
    b) Weak operating system and application default settings
    c) Common configuration and coding mistakes
    d) Protocol vulnerabilities (such as the TCP/IP stack vulnerabilities).

25. Which vulnerability assessment tools have the option to perform dangerous/destructive scans?
    a) Microsoft Baseline Security Analyzer
    b) Nessus
    c) Snort®
    d) Løphtcrack.

26. Henry and Paul are debating the purchase of a $15000 automated vulnerability assessment software package. What is the main disadvantage regarding the automated tool compared with manual assessments?

a) A result indicting a false negative may cause the organization to overreact to a security problem that does not exist.
b) False positives may require further investigation that the administrator is not qualified to perform.
c) The administrators may not be addressing the output of the automated tests.
d) Use of the tool may cost more than the cost of conducting manual assessments.

27. Which of these methods would be considered an example of passive reconnaissance?
a) Port scanning
b) Social engineering through the use of public internet sites
c) Tailgating through an identification checkpoint
d) Running HTTPRINT to determine the version of the remote web server.

28. Which of these methods would be considered an example of active reconnaissance?
a) War dialing
b) Whois lookup
c) Google hacking
d) Capturing wireless transmissions.

29. Which of these methods would help protect DNS records from access by unauthorized users?
a) Obscuring DNS registry information by using generic registration data.

b) Using Active Directory integrated zones on publicly-available DNS servers.
c) Blocking incoming UDP port 53 requests to a DMZ hosting a DNS server.
d) Using two DNS servers: an internal DNS server with internal resource records and an external DNS server with DMZ-based resource records.

30. Which of the following pieces of information can be obtained from a Whois query?
   a) Technical point of contact
   b) Private IP address block
   c) Webserver platform
   d) Uptime of server.

31. Why would an administrator block outbound "ICMP TTL Exceeded" error messages at the external gateways of the network?
   a) To reduce the workload on the routers
   b) To prevent Smurf (ICMP) attacks
   c) To prevent traceroute software from revealing information about the internal topology
   d) To prevent fragment-based denial-of-service attacks.

32. Which of the following is the most effective way to reduce the threat of social engineering?
   a) Require employees to sign an acceptable computer/internet usage policy.
   b) Prevent employees from accessing social networks from the office.

   c) Require employees to communicate using encrypted e-mails.

   d) Repeated user education on the nature of social engineering.

33. What technology is often used by employees to get access to web sites that are blocked by their corporate proxy server?
   a) DNS spoofing
   b) ARP poisoning
   c) SSL proxy
   d) Anonymous IP address allocation.

34. Why is it more difficult to sanitize information about a company that has publicly-traded stock?
   a) The company wants to promote itself as much as possible.
   b) The company must regularly submit financial information to regulatory bodies (such as the Securities and Exchange Commission (SEC)), which is then made public.
   c) It is impossible to remove cached information from search engines' databases.
   d) The company must hire a security consultant with the expertise to sanitize the information.

35. Which of the following actions can often be used as countermeasures to port scans?
   a) Blocking unassigned port traffic
   b) Disabling protocols that support cleartext authentication

c) Blocking access to TCP port 53

d) Only using encrypted services, such as SSH and SSL/TLS.

36. Assuming SNMP agent devices are IPsec-capable, why would implementing IPsec help protect SNMP agents?

   a) An insecure version of SNMPv3 is installed by default on most networking equipment.

   b) SNMPv2 sends the community name in cleartext.

   c) The method of authenticating with SNMPv1 and SNMPv2 is insecure because of its reliance on DES.

   d) SNMPv2 doesn't provide adequate integrity checks.

37. Which of the following are reasons why fragment-based port scans are often used by attackers?

   a) Firewalls may be configured for high throughput, and thus don't reassemble and inspect fragmented packets.

   b) Firewalls are always set to reject non-fragmented port scans.

   c) RFC 1121 requires that all routers pass fragmented packets.

   d) Stateful inspection firewalls will not be able to detect a fragmented attack.

38. Which of the following are recommended practices to help counteract password-guessing attacks?

   a) Ensure that UNIX passwords are stored in the /passwd file, not the shadow file.

   b) Use two-factor authentication.

c) Set a password policy with a minimum password age of 30 days.
d) Allow the use of passwords of any length in order to make them more obscure.

39. What is a common countermeasure to prevent buffer overflow exploits?
a) Ensure all input to an application is validated before being processed.
b) Enable network-based IDS software.
c) Log all attempts by users, processes or applications to elevate privilege levels.
d) Always scan new media in an antivirus system before introducing it to internal PCs.

40. Keystroke loggers are usually used in which type of attack?
a) Aggressive
b) Semantic/syntactical
c) Passive
d) Active.

41. Which of the following statements explain why hardware-based keystroke loggers are so dangerous?
a) They can inject malicious code into running applications and processes.
b) They are transparent to both the operating system and the user applications.
c) They are frequently disguised as a legitimate program patch.

d) The data they contain can be easily retrieved, even if the attacker doesn't have physical access to the machine.

42. Which of the following methods would allow an attacker to get access to the local SAM file if the attacker had physical access?
   a) Rebooting with a Linux-based floppy or CD that can read NTFS filesystems.
   b) Rebooting into Windows® using "safe mode".
   c) Compromising a system user through a browser exploit and pushing pwdump.
   d) Installing a USB-based keystroke logger on a local machine.

43. Noah, a certified penetration tester, has been asked by Company XYZ to perform a security test against the company network from an internal location. The owner of company XYZ has provided Noah with a network diagram, documentation and assistance. Which of the following would best describe the type of test that Noah is about to perform?
   a) Black box
   b) Single blind
   c) White box
   d) Gray box.

44. A malicious hacker has been trying to penetrate company XYZ from an external network location. He has tried every trick in his bag, but still is not

succeeding. From the choice presented below, which type of logical attempt is he most likely to attempt next?
a) Elevation of privileges
b) Pilfering of data
c) Denial of service
d) Installation of a backdoor.

45. The footprinting phase of a penetration test relies on a tester's ability to collect information from different sources. Only about 35% to 40% of the information collected will be from technical sources. Which of the following is a common way for a security tester to collect information during this phase?
a) Physical access
b) Exploitation of vulnerabilities
c) Social engineering
d) Cracking administrator passwords.

46. What is traceroute used for?
a) To find network gateways that are vulnerable to ICMP-based attacks.
b) To find the best path to a specified destination address.
c) To find the path a packet traveled to get to the destination address.
d) To find the initial TTL value used within a packet.

47. A normal TCP connection is always established by using what is called a TCP three-way handshake. Which of the packet sequences below would represent a normal TCP connection establishment?

a) SYN, SYN/ACK, ACK
b) SYN, PSH, ACK
c) SYN, ACK
d) SYN, RST, SYN/ACK.

48. Which of the following scan types would be the least accurate, considering that many other network conditions could indicate that a port is open when it might not actually be?
   a) Vanilla TCP port scan
   b) UDP port scan
   c) Half-open scan
   d) Inverse TCP scan.

49. In an ACK flag scan, the target host is sent TCP packets with the ACK flag set, and the reply is then analyzed. Which of the following items within the response packets would be used to determine if the port was open on the remote host?
   a) The Time To Live (TTL) field
   b) The source port
   c) The destination port
   d) The packet fragment indicator.

50. Which of the following statements would be true when referring to stream ciphers?
   a) Stream ciphers encrypt one bit or character at a time.
   b) Stream ciphers commonly use a frequently repeated key stream to encrypt the message.
   c) Stream ciphers impose a high computational overhead on systems.

d) Stream ciphers can only be implemented in software.

51. Bob has just produced a very detailed penetration testing report for his client. Bob wishes to ensure that the report will not be changed in storage or in transit. What would be the best tool Bob could use to assure the integrity of the information and detect any changes that might have happened to the report while being transmitted or stored?
    a) A symmetric encryption algorithm
    b) An asymmetric encryption algorithm
    c) A hashing algorithm
    d) A stream-based algorithm.

52. Nathalie is exclusively making use of a public key cryptographic system to communicate with her peers. She would like to send information to Bob, while protecting the confidentiality of the content being sent over the public network. Which key will she use to encrypt the message content, before sending it?
    a) Bob's private key
    b) A shared secret key
    c) Bob's public key
    d) Nathalie's private key.

53. Vulnerabilities scanners have large databases of known vulnerabilities and exposures that exist within a very large number of operating systems and applications. What is one of the biggest disadvantages of automated security scanners when remaining stealthy is an issue?

a) They can only test IP-based vulnerabilities and will be detected by an IDS.
b) They will only work if the correct ports are open on the firewall, and traffic on those ports will increase.
c) The scanner might require a large amount of memory, disk space and processing power, and cause the system to slow down or malfunction.
d) A very large amount of traffic will be sent against the target.

54. Julius has been hired to perform a test on company XYZ networks. Julius knows that company XYZ has a large team of security administrators, who are very proactive in their security approach. Most likely, there are some Intrusion Detection Systems (IDSs) in place that would quickly identify Julius's IP address, and he would then be blocked from accessing the network he is supposed to test. Which of the following would be the most practical and easiest solution Julius could take to avoid having his IP address identified and then blocked?

a) Using public key encryption (the IDS cannot decipher encrypted traffic and determine the source of the probes).
b) Using Secure Socket Layer (SSL) to shield the intruder from the IDS and hide the signatures of the attack software.
c) Using only computers that have their IP address spoofed to IP addresses within the local network (the IDS will identify all the traffic as legitimate internal traffic and not log the traffic or alert the administrator).

d) Using an internet anonymizer instead of connecting directly to the target (the anonymizer will shield the real source of the probes and, if it is blocked, can simply be changed to another proxy).

55. One of the last steps taken by an attacker will be to configure a method of permanent access to a compromised system. However, the installation of a backdoor, new processes, and changes to key files could be very quickly detected by an administrator. Which tool would assist the attacker in preventing the administrator from detecting changes to files, new processes that are running, or other signs that the system might have been compromised?
    a) A Trojan horse
    b) A rootkit
    c) A logic bomb
    d) A privilege escalation tool.

56. Mae is a keen system administrator. She constantly monitors the mailing list for best practices that are being used out in the field. On the servers that she maintains, Mae has renamed the administrator account to avoid abuse from crackers. However, she found out that it was possible, using the "sid2user" tool, to find the new name she chose for the administrator account. Mae does not understand; she has *not* shared this name with anyone. How did the name get out? What is the most likely reason?
    a) Her system admin account may have been compromised.

b) Renaming the administrator account does not change the SID.
c) She is running an unpatched system.
d) Someone used social engineering to manipulate her.

Answers

1. C	20. B	39. A
2. C	21. D	40. C
3. D	22. C	41. B
4. A	23. A	42. A
5. D	24. A	43. D
6. D	25. B	44. C
7. C	26. B	45. C
8. C	27. B	46. C
9. B	28. A	47. A
10. C	29. D	48. B
11. C	30. A	49. A
12. B	31. C	50. A
13. A	32. D	51. C
14. B	33. C	52. C
15. C	34. B	53. D
16. C	35. A	54. D
17. A	36. B	55. B
18. C	37. A	56. B.
19. D	38. B	

REFERENCES

This is a partial list of references that a penetration tester may wish to review as a part of their development:

- *ISO/IEC 27001:2005 – Information technology – Security techniques – Information security management systems – Requirements*

- *ISO/IEC 27002:2005 – Information technology – Security techniques – Code of practice for information security management*

- *ISO/IEC 27005:2011 – Information technology – Security techniques – Information security risk management*

- *ISO/IEC 31000:2009 – Risk management – Principles and guidelines*

- *ISO/IEC 20000-1:2011 – Information technology – Service management – Part 1: Service management system requirements*

- *NIST SP 800-115 – Technical Guide to Information Security Testing and Assessment* (2008)

- *NIST SP 800-81 Revision 1 – Secure Domain Name System (DNS) Deployment Guide* (2009)

- *NIST SP 800-53A Revision 1 – Guide for Assessing the Security Controls in Federal Information Systems and Organizations, Building Effective Security Assessment Plans* (2010)

- *NIST SP 800-41 Revision 1 – Guidelines on Firewalls and Firewall Policy* (2002).

ITG RESOURCES

IT Governance Ltd. sources, creates and delivers products and services to meet the real-world, evolving IT governance needs of today's organizations, directors, managers and practitioners. The ITG website (*www.itgovernance.co.uk*) is the international one-stop-shop for corporate and IT governance information, advice, guidance, books, tools, training and consultancy.

http://www.itgovernance.co.uk/penetration-testing-packages.aspx is the page on our website for resources relevant to this book.

Other Websites

Books and tools published by IT Governance Publishing (ITGP) are available from all business booksellers and are also immediately available from the following websites:

www.itgovernance.co.uk/catalog/355 provides information and online purchasing facilities for every currently available book published by ITGP.

http://www.itgovernance.eu is our euro-denominated website which ships from Benelux and has a growing range of books in European languages other than English.

www.itgovernanceusa.com is a US$-based website that delivers the full range of IT Governance products to North America, and ships from within the continental US.

www.itgovernanceasia.com provides a selected range of ITGP products specifically for customers in South Asia.

www.27001.com is the IT Governance Ltd. website that deals specifically with information security management, and ships from within the continental US.

Pocket Guides

For full details of the entire range of pocket guides, simply follow the links at *www.itgovernance.co.uk/publishing.aspx*.

Toolkits

ITG's unique range of toolkits includes the IT Governance Framework Toolkit, which contains all the tools and guidance that you will need in order to develop and implement an appropriate IT governance framework for your organization. Full details can be found at *www.itgovernance.co.uk/products/519*.

For a free paper on how to use the proprietary Calder-Moir IT Governance Framework, and for a free trial version of the toolkit, see *www.itgovernance.co.uk/calder_moir.aspx*.

There is also a wide range of toolkits to simplify implementation of management systems, such as an ISO/IEC 27001 ISMS or a BS25999 BCMS, and these can all be viewed and purchased online at: *http://www.itgovernance.co.uk/catalog/1*.

Best Practice Reports

ITG's range of Best Practice Reports is now at *www.itgovernance.co.uk/best-practice-reports.aspx*. These offer you essential, pertinent, expertly researched information on a number of key issues including Web 2.0 and Green IT.

Training and Consultancy

IT Governance also offers training and consultancy services across the entire spectrum of disciplines in the information governance arena. Details of training courses can be accessed at *www.itgovernance.co.uk/training.aspx* and descriptions of our consultancy services can be found at *http://www.itgovernance.co.uk/consulting.aspx*. Why not contact us to see how we could help you and your organization?

Newsletter

IT governance is one of the hottest topics in business today, not least because it is also the fastest moving, so what better way to keep up than by subscribing to ITG's free monthly newsletter *Sentinel*? It provides monthly updates and resources across the whole spectrum of IT governance subject matter, including risk management, information security, ITIL and IT service management, project governance, compliance and so much more. Subscribe for your free copy at: *www.itgovernance.co.uk/newsletter.aspx*.